Arnaud van der Veere

Muay Thai

Meyer & Meyer Sport

Muay Thai

Arnaud van der Veere
Maidenhead: Meyer & Meyer Sport (UK) Ltd., 2012
ISBN: 978-1-84126-328-1

© 2012 by Meyer & Meyer Verlag, Aachen
Auckland, Beirut, Budapest, Cairo, Cape Town, Dubai, Indianapolis,
Kindberg, Maidenhead, Sydney, Olten, Singapore, Tehran, Toronto
Member of the World
Sport Publishers' Association (WSPA)
www.w-s-p-a.org
Printed by: B.O.S.S Druck und Medien GmbH
ISBN: 978-1-84126-328-1
E-Mail: info@m-m-sports.com
www.m-m-sports.com

CONTENTS

FOREWORD

When I was asked to write the Foreword to this book, I honestly broke out in a sweat. I can talk very well, and I am a man of action. But writing? No, I am not a writer and I will never be. Yet I could definitely not decline Arnaud van der Veere's request. Anyone who knows me and my long kickboxing history knows that I pretty much live for the sport. And that is why I always like to participate in everything that makes a positive contribution to it, be it Radio, TV or Newspapers.

This is also the case for the book "Muay Thai" by Arnaud van der Veere, and that is why I chose to sit down behind my dusty and shaky writing table. I do it because I saw immediately that the book "fills a need." It is clearly written and accessible to anyone and should stand in the bookshelf of anyone who is serious about the sport. All techniques of kickboxing are very well described by Van der Veere on the basis of clear images. Of course I know better than anyone that most of the work is carried out in the gym, but even in kickboxing a bit of theory cannot hurt.

In short, as a multiple European kickboxing champion and owner of – in all modesty – the largest and most beautiful martial arts center in the Netherlands, I can heartily recommend this book. And if I recommend a book, then that means something. Not only that I am far from being a born writer, I am also not really the most avid reader. Even at my "old age" I still prefer to spend my time in the gym.

For "Muay Thai" by Arnaud van der Veere, however, I made an exception.

Jan Oosterbaan

www.oosterbaangym.nl

1   THE SPORT OF MUAY THAI

After years of research, it was discovered that martial arts originally came from India. The roots are thought to be Kalaripayattu, the mother of all martial arts. This dance-like fighting form is not to be used in combat or competition in the ring. Kalaripayattu is currently still practiced in Kerala, a beautiful state located in southern part of India. The legend of this practice begins in the Ramayana, where men were meant to play a part in the heavenly battle between the gods. In the pictures of the Ramayana, there are many battles between gods and supernatural beings. These battles contain the basic fighting forms of Kalaripayattu.

Travelers, monks, gurukal of Kalaripayattu, the army and Ramayana figures have transported the soul and movements of the art all over Asia. Each country took a part of it and formulated its own principles and rules. Because of this, there is great variety within the martial arts. According to legend, Bodhidharma needed monks to stay awake during meditation and created a series of exercises also based on Kalaripayattu. These movements seemed to be the origin of Shaolin Kung Fu. The art then was introduced to Thailand. In Thailand, Muay Thai is a practical application of these actions in real combat.

The increasing number of training classes and gyms that exist today may be proof that people today want a total martial art workout to relax the body from stress and fatigue. Muay Thai provides the opportunity to train safely and, if desired, to also train or fight competitively with a partner or opponent.

In the past, the world of Muay Thai was a men-only world. However, since 1990 an increasing number of women have participated in, and even teach, classes every day. In my lessons and shop, the number of active women is still increasing. It is positive to see that they take the martial arts serious and live accordingly.

Dutch Muay Thai was practiced only by a lucky few (amongst them was Arnaud van der Veere). In the beginning of the 1970s and '80s, the Netherlands was the center of Europe for competition, with Amsterdam known as the "fighting city." Great names arose from the little country.

The first person to introduce full contact fights in the Netherlands was Charles Dumerniet. Thanks to him, the Chakuriki style and its creator Thom Harinck rose to fame. The "red devils" took the full contact "world" by storm with their own mixed fighting style and red kimonos.

K-1, a Japanese-based organization, made the sport a commercial success. They took the competitive element of the sport to the extreme and maximized professionalism. Behind the master of this organization, Kazuyoshi Ishii, stood a number of famous Dutch trainers, including Jan Plas and Johan Vos. Fighting was combined with show and glamour, making it a fun night out for the family.

K-1 stands for karate, Kung Fu, kickboxing, and many other martial arts to practice combat-like situations in the ring under a tournament system. The system provided the first commercial place for fighters to perform to their top of abilities and earn a good living. At times more than 80,000 spectators watch the performances of the "gladiators." After the great successes, K-1 got competition from new ring styles like Shooto, cage fights, and free fight.

Moving to the professional realm changed much within the martial arts. Trainers are forced to take students to the edges of their abilities, top athletes have to live a disciplined lifestyle, trainers must continue to be educated and study the science of movements, coaches and all others must be able to assist in first aid, dieting, weight control, weight training, etc. In the old days, there were masters and students. A master was considered to know all. In the current situation, there are no masters any longer. A trainer is the person who works with the fighter to improve his or her skills, help him or her reach maximum abilities and help him or her move on to the next level. No longer do we work with color belts or fake diplomas. Both trainer and student need to perform and prove who and what they are.

To open a gym is no small matter anymore. To rent a place and start teaching is only possible at the beginner's level. To bring students to a higher level in competition, good equipment plays an important role. Competition or recreational training programs are a matter of planning. I use Dutch Muay Thai to treat students' addiction, mental problems, physical disabilities, and more. Students need to study their sport and prepare for training. Books and visual media are a great help to everyone. This book and available visual media are your guides in the ring sports.

2   HISTORY OF THAILAND AND MUAY THAI

The history of Muay Thai is bonded to the country Thailand. When the Thai (also known as the Dai in China's province Yunan, where the Thai originated) invaded the northern part of Thailand, the country was already occupied by the Mon and Khmer. The Mon reached the central part of Thailand around the first century after leaving Burma and settled down. The Khmer came from the area now called Cambodia and inhabited the eastern part of Thailand.

Under the Mon, the kingdom of Dvaravati became powerful and rich. The capital was based where Nakhom Phanom is now situated, a bit west of Bangkok (Krung Thep). They promoted Theravada Buddhism and created new religious sites. In the 11th century, the Khmer attacked the central low lands and conquered the Mon. The capital of the country became Lopburi. It was around this time that the Thai entered the area of what would become Siam.

In 651 AD, the Thai founded an autonomous kingdom in the Chinese Yunnan area called Nanchao. Continuous pressure by the Chinese army irritated most of the Thai and they decided to move away from the territory. The people then moved toward the Mekong. They explored the region, and some stayed while others moved on. During their travel, they encountered different enemies and were involved in many wars. During war and traveling, their medical knowledge reached a high level, and even today this knowledge is still used in many traditional practices.

When on the move, a warrior needs to be inventive and adaptive. The Thai learned to use many different weapons and took over the weapons and tactics of their opponents. In doing so, they developed a warrior system of armed and unarmed combat. When they took warriors in captivity, the Thai placed them in their ranks and learned their ways of fighting. After learning, they improved or changed the techniques and methods until they fit their specific demands and needs.

During the 12th century, the Thai invaded Burma, now called Myanmar, from the north and settled there. Today the tribe that settled in this area is called Shan (Shanstate). In light of history, the Shan are still more connected with the Thai than the Burmese. On the way to Burma, some Thai groups separated and founded city states called Muang (one named Fang still exists).

To live a relatively peaceful life, the Thai had to pay tribute to the Khmer. Increasing pressure from the Khmer and the ever-rising cost forced some Muang to cooperate and turn against the Khmer. In 1238, a group of Muang organized a collective battle against the Khmer and defeated them. The battlefield was near the first capital of Siam (Thailand) Sukhothai. In 1256, Kublai Khan swept his armies over the province of Nanchao and the Thai fled, seeking refuge in the new kingdom of Sukhothai.

This resulted in the establishment of a new kingdom and the designation of Sukhothai as the capital. The united army spread its influence over a large area now known as Burma, Malaysia and Singapore. Originally, the Thai were called

Siamese which refers to the Chinese word "Shan" that means gold or yellow. Due to this, the Shan in Burma kept the name in honor of the Thai founders.

From 1275 (until 1317) the Thai were governed by the great Ram Khamhaeng who laid down the fundamentals of the Thai alphabet. Thai is based on Sanskrit and Pali. The founding of a national language created a feeling of unity and nationalism. Ram Khamhaeng was a true promoter of the arts, among which was the art of Muay Thai.

After his death, the Ayutthaya period began in 1350 and lasted until 1767. The new capital of Ayutthaya was located on the Chao Phraya river near today's Bangkok. The Ayutthaya period was marked by the increased influence of the Hindu Khmer and the treatment of the kings as half gods. The founder of Ayutthaya, king U'Thong took for himself the name Ramathibodi (1350-1369).

During the Ayutthaya period, Siam was in a constant state of war with Burma. The Burmese conquered the citizens of Ayutthaya in 1569 and ruled them until 1584. This period was ended by the warrior king Naresuan. This king was an excellent Muay Thai fighter, warlord, and tactician. As a strategist, he is considered to have written the first book on the origin, fighting methods and art of Muay Thai. King Naresuan is a national hero who freed Siam from the Burmese invaders.

In 1603, the Dutch were the first to set up a diplomatic mission in Siam, and the Thai chose Holland as the first diplomatic settlement in Europe. The understanding between the two nations is still at a high level even today. Considering its history, it is not strange that in Muay Thai Holland is number one in the heavyweight world ranking list and next to Thailand in lighter weight classes.

The Dutch were the first to establish a diplomatic mission in 1604 in Siam's capital. In reverse, the Thai started a mission in Amsterdam, the Netherlands as the first settlement in Europe. A great boxer of that time Nai Khanom Dtom made history. In a challenge for his freedom, he competed with 10 Burmese warriors and defeated them all. After the fights, he was released for his courage and honored for his skills. Muay Thai flourished under the reign of the "tiger king" Pra Chao Sua, who was not only a skilled fighter but also a man who studied and recorded all details of the art. He was known for traveling in disguise to all parts of his kingdom to take part in competitions. During the time of peace, warriors and civil servants had to stay in shape with physical practice. Muay Thai became an important part of all training and recreation. Non-military citizens were also interested in the art.

Slowly, the interest of the citizens increased for public performances and training of Muay Thai. A competition started between army, civil servants and the other citizens of Siam.

King Pra Chao Sua wrote an important book on Muay Thai that is still today seen as the "bible" of Muay Thai. It is written in Thai and had many editions, but it was not translated until recent times. The competition rules of Muay Thai were very simple but straightforward. Hands needed to be wrapped with horse leather, cotton, or other textiles. After wrapping, the fighters dipped their hands in a bucket filled with glue mixed with sand or glass. The fights did not have a time limit; they took as long as needed for one of the fighters to start bleeding. The referee than decided whether the fight was ended or would continue. Muay Thai in that time included throws, punches, kicks, elbows, etc. There were no weight classes – everyone competed against everyone. Luckily for the Thai, there were not large differences in weights. But the system was very tough and some people died in battle. In 1930, the rules were radically changed to fit international boxing rules.

The target of the Thai Sports Commission was to accept Muay Thai as an Olympic sport. But to reach that goal most of the original components of Muay Thai, like the Ram Muay (the heart of the Muay Thai dance rituals) were cut away by foreign influences. Olympics in that time were dominated by the so-called Western upper-class and they ruled the sport as uncivilized and unsophisticated. Traditional English Boxing was only accepted after a long struggle of English lords against the Olympic Committee. Even boxing was still under strong scrutiny by many "civilized" citizens. Fighting in general was seen as barbarian. The general concept was that only soldiers needed to fight when on the battlefield, fighting was not sport nor entertainment. Considering this point of view among others, the Asian population as a whole was considered inferior to the West. We have to see all of these issues through the light of the colonial perspective of most of the Western (European) nations who ruled Asia. The result of these critiques was that the Thai changed the rules and regulations and made Muay Thai into a sport. Weight classes were introduced, along with gloves, five rounds (each three minutes with a two-minute interval), a knockout/knock down ruling and a referee/judging system.

A period of change occurred. Old style fighters could not compete anymore and had to withdraw from competition. A significant decrease of fighters followed. But thanks to the heart of the Thai and love of the art a new breed of fighter arose from the camps and slowly competition grew again. However, when fighting under original rules or the Chachuap rules the Thai and Burmese will prove their superior quality again and again.

To promote Muay Thai worldwide, the Thai Tourist Organization joined teams with the newly founded Boxing Counsel to attract foreigners to learn the art of Muay Thai and get acquainted with the locally famous Muay Thai fighters. Dutch and Japanese fighters were among the largest groups to show interest.

The most famous stadiums in Bangkok are Lumpini, Radjadamnern, Samrong, Channel 7, and more recently Pattaya Stadium. Fights are held on a regular basis in all of these stadiums; often more than three nights a week. Due to this and the nearly daily broadcast of the fights, the sport stays popular even amongst young people. In addition, movies like Ong-Bak, have given the Thai a national boost of energy and pride concerning their national sport.

In the USA, Muay Thai was learned by Marines and ex-marines who stayed in Thailand during and after the Vietnam War. But many Americans prefer sports with a show-like character and semi-contact competition. The only full contact

competitions that were scored were full contact taekwondo and the World Karate Association style, which allowed only low kicks. One of karate's most famous fighters ever was from the Los Angeles area (though originally from Mexico), Benny "The Jet" Urquidez. He only fought once against a European (the Dutch champion Ivan Sprang) under American style rules.

In Europe, Muay Thai gained popularity when the Indonesians and Dutch learned the art during their stay in the war prison camps and after their liberation. They took the art back to Holland. The French also learned the art through immigrants, students who came over to Paris. In the '60s, a group of interested students started the Circle Muay Thai with headquarters in Paris. This small organization promoted Muay Thai among their own people and other Asians. Competition was limited and very few foreigners had entrance. In Europe, countries like Holland, Germany, France, the United Kingdom, Spain, and Switzerland had competitors. The author of this book joined this group at the age of eight, competed for the first time in Thailand at the age of fifteen, and continued competing until 1991.

In Holland, Muay Thai was introduced through kickboxing and free fight competitions. Charles Dumerniet organized this "anything goes" full contact competitions that gained international attention because of their new border-crossing fights. A trainer named Thom Harinck started his own style called Chakuriki. Dressed in impressive red suits, fighters equipped with street fighting techniques competed and won most of the fights. The first encounter of this group with original Muay Thai fighters in Bangkok ended all in lost fights in round 1 or 2 knockouts. However, the Dutch competitors learned and took all techniques from the Thai. Daring as they were, another group was formed with fighters from gyms like Mejiro Gym (Jan Plas) and Vos Gym (Johan Vos). Still the Thai were stronger, but they needed more rounds and had to compete fiercely to win. Many fighters from Holland followed, and they competed and also won. Some became national heroes in Thailand, such as Ramon Dekker and Rob Kaman. Dutch competitors often proved to be too strong for the Thai. However competitions between Dutch and Thai are seen as main events all over the world.

Arnaud van der Veere, the author of this book, competed all over Thailand between 1975 (long before the first Dutch group arrived) and 1991. He fought in the different styles of Muay Thai, such as Kachuab, Burmese Boxing, Muay Boran, and got his lessons in Krabi Krabong from the (female) masters of Rose Garden in Bangkok. Due to his white blond hair and iron blue eyes, he became the face of the Dutch Muay Thai Fighters. His book on kickboxing/Muay Thai, published in

1984, was the "bible" for fighters and trainers due to its comprehensive, factual and easy-to-understand content. Most fighters and trainers got their education from that book as it was used by many groups for years as part of their trainers' education programs. Arnaud van der Veere is considered one of the founders of Dutch Muay Thai and is currently chairman of the FIMTT, Federation of Independent Muay Thai Trainers around the world. All members are requested or have passed heavy examinations .

Kickboxing came from Japan. Japan was not allowed by the Thai to carry the name Muay Thai anymore after a corruption scheme. Some Japanese fight coordinators invited many Thai to compete in Japan and then paid them to lose. This was a blow to the national pride of Thailand, and they warned Japan never to use the name Muay Thai again. The main person to introduce kickboxing in Europe was Jan Plas of Mejiro Gym, a karate specialist who had a wide interest in fighting as a ring sport.

The art has spread all over the world. However, many "teachers" think they know how the art is practiced but do not, and even more created "their own styles." Now many organizations have their own World Champions or have created other fancy titles. In fact, not one of these titles is worth the paper it is written on. Some made K1 the tournament of world champions but due to the sometimes fixed pre-matches and the fact it is not a completely open form of competition, it cannot be considered a real world title. The K1 "heavy weight" competition is considered the real world title, the competition is fierce and the selection is not made based on entertainment. It is still not open for everyone.

Perhaps one day the Thai government will feel it is necessary to develop a certification training program that standardizes and recognizes official Muay Thai practices. Doing this would allow potential students to choose a proper school where they would get authentic training in true Muay Thai practices and not those of a school just wishing to make money off by awarding fake certificates and titles.

3   PHILOSOPHY OF THE FIGHTER

First of all, I have to set something straight. The word "fighter" is considered negative in most common language usage, but fighting is positive attitude. Remember when someone told you that it was worth it to fight for your life, your work, your relationship? We all need to be a fighter in life; nothing comes for granted. Fighting is a very important word that equals determination. In this book, we want to make clear what we consider to be a fighter and show how we consider it to be a positive attitude toward a serious role in society. We all want to make a better, positive society.

What do we consider a fighter? Is it only a person who is involved in competitions or also the one who is involved in training in the gym? In my opinion, anyone who is seriously working out in training at least three to four times a week is a "fighter," whether male or female. As a fighter, it is important to have a training philosophy, something I call the "way of the warrior."

The main goal of a fighter is not to fight the opponent or partner. The goal is to excel, to become better at every training session, become more skillful, develop more power and a better physical condition. Each training session is a chance to be a better person than before.

A real fighter works on his or her inner peace and balance. The fighter must be focused on the perfection of techniques, breathing, focus , timing, food, lifestyle. All of this is will make him or her better in what he or she is doing. Meditation is also one of the most important parts of a good fighter.

Most people think that meditation is only done by sitting and breathing – controlling the mind, the thoughts. But a fighter meditates in activity. During a workout, the focus of the mind, the perfection of breathing, the reflexes and drills, are part of the meditation of the fighter. When working out, the mind turns to an inward-oriented position and, while the body is moving under the commands of trainer or task, the fighter's mind is no longer busy with the thoughts and problems of the everyday life. These problems vanish and become one with the overall exercise of mind and body.

The real fighter is peaceful, not aggressive, humble in attitude and behavior, artistic in mind and practice, and a sociable person. The fighter is thankful and appreciates life as given, and is willing to share with others. In many ways, I like to compare a good fighter with an ancient "mandarin" of China. The mandarin was a person willing to develop skills to serve the people and able to express himself and convince others to follow the right path in life. Real fighters are very important social role models. In our changing society, the ring fighter becomes a star and needs to be aware of his place by behaving accordingly.

4 DIFFERENCES BETWEEN EASTERN AND WESTERN FIGHTERS

While traveling through Asia and Europe, I saw many differences between the fighters. In the past, these differences were large, and customs were also much more different. But over the decades, so many people have been traveling around and economics have changed that it seems the differences are fading away, but are they?

The differences are deeply hidden in the brain and psyche of us all. Western people are physically different from Asians and the way we think is also different. At first glance, many Westerners appear to have larger, stronger bodies when compared to most Asians. In addition, their approach to language is rather different as Westerners tend to speak more directly and to the point, while Asians' language is a bit more indirect in its intention.

When we look at the skills Asians developed for the fighting arts, they developed the "art of war" and are tough in battle or competition. Western ways of fighting are direct, powerful and not gentle at all. Asians play with the forces, while Westerners use the forces. When we fight, there is a need to combine these two ways.

Problem solving is addressed in different ways. Many Asians look at problems from all sides and angles before making a decision. Westerners tend to look for solutions to problems immediately, often times without taking proper time to evaluate the situation with the idea that they can just try a different solution if the first fails.

Asians train in a different way. An Asian fighter, who typically values tradition and proper technique in a way that Westerners do not, follows orders; he obeys what is said by the trainer, no complaints, no demands, he just follows what he is told. Westerners typically like to enjoy the training. Many want it to be a social event where you can talk and have fun. They also like constant change. Westerners, who typically value being unique and independent in a way that Asians do not, often do not follow the orders of the trainers, and as a result, they do things a little differently, and they always put their own creativity in the exercise. Both ways can deliver good results.

Due to their dichotomous mindset, Westerners tend to have difficulty getting into a meditative mood. However, Asians, who were raised in a more holistic mindset, find it is easier to accomplish this task. A Western fighter is able to relax faster and

easier than an Asian, likely due to his or her "independent" mentality. If pressure is put on an Asian fighter, he will try to perform even better as he is better able to be patient; but if pressure is put on a Westerner, if his first few options fail, he will often quit, stop the training or go somewhere else as he is more impatient when not getting the results he seeks.

In Asia, we can separate fighters into two categories (remember, I am only generalizing to make some ideas clearer): the fighters who can take a punch and the fighters who cannot. In Asia, the Muay Thai fighters are so tough that they can take a punch because they are trained to do so. Westerners can often take a punch, or even a lot of them.

Of course, there are many more differences. This book is about fighters, which is why I have focused on some differences related to fighting. The purpose of the comparison is to show that it is not the way you take to reach the target as long as you are able to achieve the final goal – win the fight and/or become a better person.

5   WHY TO TRAIN AS MUCH AS POSSIBLE

Training is the programming of the body and mind. When you want to become better or learn something well, you have to practice. The more you train, the better you become. Training demands discipline, and regular practice requires a focused mind and a proper lifestyle.

Training as much as possible does not demand a 100% intensity every time; that is impossible. Your body needs time to recuperate. Some days, you should train at full intensity but other days you should lower the percentage. Most weeks can be divided into:

2 days at maximum (seldom 100%) intensity
2 days at 70-80%
2 days at 50-60%
1 day at 20-30%

This way you are able to keep full concentration, give the body time to recover, and allow your mind time to absorb the technical aspects of each training.

A training session is normally between 1 and 2 hours. Your body is able to work at a maximum intensity for around 1 hour. This implies that full intensity training must be shorter than low intensity. The minimum workout time to be effective for the body is 30 minutes.

Mental and tactical training can last longer as often the training contains some discussions and argumentation of principles. The physical exertion is low, and the body is able to continue training longer.

Often fighters train using long distance running. This is a method of training that I sincerely doubt is of any use to a martial artist or other fighter. Our bodies are in need of explosive actions. After each series of explosive actions, we need to recover and maybe defend. Training for a long distance sport requires different body and mind sets.

In conclusion, training is important to set the body and mind in harmony and make them work together as a perfect "machine." The more often you train, the better the tuning. The intensity of the trainings must differ. Fighting is based on observation, reflexes, and the ability to read the opponent. In tournaments, we have to add the ability to fight strategically to this list.

6   DIFFERENCES IN FIGHTING BETWEEN MEN AND WOMEN

Men and women are different, we all know that. In the fighting arts, we have to consider one important factor that makes a big difference between male and female: testosterone!

Testosterone is the male hormone that is responsible for strength, aggression, and everything that makes a man a male. The level of testosterone in women is much lower.

Testosterone makes a difference not only on a physical level, but also on a psychological level concerning state of mind. In my opinion, women need to receive parts of the training in different ways than men. For instance, breasts make it harder to closely defend the upper body. However, women have a different hip/leg structure and thus can kick easier than men. The differences go on and on.

For a trainer, it is very important to realize the differences between men and women when preparing for competition, but it is even more important to understand the differences while teaching standard or special classes.

Many men want to keep women out of the martial arts, though I do not understand why. Are men scared for women? Scared to lose control? I always wonder about the reasons behind men telling me that women do not belong in

the ring. How many men actually still defend their wives in battle? Imagine how much comfort it will be to know the woman is able to defend herself and her family. I am strongly in favor of a large increase of women in our sports.

In conclusion, it will take many books to cover all differences between men and women. In fighting arts, we need to look at the practical sides of training. The physical differences urge a more pragmatic approach. Women are important for the growth of the sport, so trainers must adjust accordingly.

7 HOW FIGHTING HELPS WITH PSYCHOLOGICAL PROBLEMS

Humans are survivors. We are born to struggle, and our basic desire is to hunt. We used to run after animals to get food. This concept is still in our genes. Most people have suppressed their inner feelings since youth due to our current society. Our education and environment do not allow us to express violence, attitude, anger, or even stress properly. All of these are suppressed in order to cooperate efficiently with others. The mass society is confusing to us. Many people feel the pressure of their everyday life at work, home, and even in the street. We need to avoid conflict. When we avoid conflicts, we need to find alternative ways to release the energy built up inside our head and body.

In martial arts, we create the image of a fight. We help to express the inner fear, anger, and stress. The concept of (Dutch) Muay Thai is the use of explosive actions to release the maximum amount of stress from the body. It is proven that when using endurance training most people will not be released of all stress. The main reason is that stress is explosive in nature. When a person gets angry, he/she starts shouting, making explosive movements, hitting things, and maybe even throwing things.

In our society, stress is the root of many psychological problems. Martial arts need stress to perform effectively. The right combination of working out stress and relaxation makes a good training. During each training, a fighter learns to use explosive power to stress the muscles, focus the soul, and concentrate energy in explosive movements to relax directly after the moment of impact.

A fighter learns to use stress as a positive technique during training, to control emotions such as fear, anger and aggression, and instead turns them into a positive-controlled movement with a focused mind. This change is important to fighting most psychological problems at the basic level. Of course, when a person has serious problems, the need of more professional help is important.

8   THE 30-MINUTE CONCEPT

Lessons, in general, are more than one hour. The body needs time to warm up and cool down. A training session is built in different phases:

- Warm-up
- Technical phase
- Reaction phase
- Speed phase
- Cardio phase
- Cool-down

Warm-up — This develops the relationship between the muscle and joint structures. It improves total muscle blood circulation, coordination, flexibility and therefore prepares the participant for things to come.

Technical phase — Learning proper techniques starts with single or double techniques and slowly we add new items and combinations to them.

Combination — A number of techniques that follow in a logical order. For example, left and right punch, and left low kick.

Time routine — A series of techniques that follow without a specified number but are instead limited by time. For example, 2 minutes of punching, without counting.

Reaction phase — The participant reacts to specific commands given by the instructor. The object is to stimulate high mental awareness and fast neurological response.

Speed phase — The participant tries to complete a given number of kicks, punches or combinations in the fastest time possible.

Cardio phase — The participant tries to complete a high number of kicks, punches, or combinations in a given amount of time.

Cool-down — This phase is used to gradually bring the heart rate and circulation back to normal. The cool-down mostly consists of low dynamic stretching.

Interval phase — A combination of fast activity regulated by a time limit (or distance) and a period (always time-depended) of relaxation/slow down. The combination of any high intensity workout and rest or slow down is called the interval phase.

During the 30-minute workout, music is an important stimulation. Music is divided in beats per minute = BPM. The higher the BPM, the faster the music tempo. Some prefer a tempo change in the warm-up, and thus adjust the BPM. During the bag workout, an increase in BPM is advisable. In the cool-down phase, decrease the BPM.

9   WARMING UP

Exercises like stretching are not standard for Thai but are necessary for most others. Because the Thai live in a warm climate, the muscle tone and blood flow through the muscles is different from people living in other parts of the world. A Thai has also been influenced by the sport since birth. TV, markets and all festivals expose them to Muay Thai. The collective mentality of the Thai is influenced by Muay Thai itself. It seems that the daily display on TV, newspapers in the temples, and in schools leaves a permanent image. It is called the "land of smiles and friendly people" because they are able to divert negative energy in their own cultural heritage. Today, we see that fewer Thai practice the sport and, as a possible result, aggressive and unfriendly behavior is on the rise.

Warming up is very important for all sports, especially in the martial arts. For example, stretching, flexibility, the training of all basic movements, power and conditioning are strongly advised for all. To maintain happiness and interest in the sport, we need to vary all warm-up exercises and use our imaginations to create fun in the sport for both student and teacher.

In this book, I outline a few warm-up techniques. To start safely and secure, keep a few basic rules in mind.

1.   Do not overstretch nor stretch hard when the body is still cool. Never stretch too long.
2.   Use a combination of active and passive stretching (active is when you maintain a continuous movement to stretch the muscle, and passive is when you stay in a stretched position for a longer period of time).
3.   Use rope jumping (or other apparatus) for conditioning and warm-up. The use of equipment improves your range of exercises and makes training more fun.
4.   Combine with free jumping and bending exercises.

In the past, warm-up sessions could take up to 30 or more minutes. This is no longer the case. The modern way of warming up is by using short and dynamic movements to increase blood flow to the muscles. After a good warm-up, start the main training activity. This is called sport specific training, and it delivers faster results.

The warm-up should take around 10 minutes. All movements target flexibility and blood circulation. We work out in what I call "CNN style" (CNN once did a research study that showed that people in a super market have an attention span of maximum 3 minutes before becoming impatient. During my lessons I have found this to be a correct assumption and that is why I have called the short concentration span and my reaction to it the "CNN method"). Each exercise takes only 5 to 10 repetitions before moving to the next and so on. The reason for such fast change is to prepare the participant for the fast changes in moves during a sparring or fighting match. Kickboxing and Thai boxing are impulsive and explosive sports, and the muscles/nerves need to be prepared for the movements.

1

2

3

Basic stance for warming up

Spread legs wider

Move down left leg and support with the hands

4

Move to the right and support with the hands

5

Bend over to stretch lower back

6

Stretch to left leg (both in active and passive way)

7

Also stretch to the right leg several times

8

From basic stance turn to relay back muscles

9

Turn the other side for same effect

10

Stretch the triceps muscles in arm

11

Turn the other side for same effect

12

Stretch the leg muscles

13

Same but seen from the side

14

Full stretch, nose to knees

15

Stretch of quadriceps

16

Same but seen from the side

17

Same but seen from the side

18

Side stretch left

19

Side stretch right

20

Triceps stretch

21

Side leg stretch front

10   STANDING AND WALKING

The basics of every sport are grounded in the way we walk and stand. All martial arts have their own basic positions from which they perform all movements. Basic standing and walking are important and must be trained daily even when you reach an advanced level. Physiotherapists and physical therapy currently focus on the improvement of core stability for all patients. In martial arts, the training is based on the balance and improvement of this core stability as a major part of every training session. Muay Thai is an excellent way to hone and excel in balance and power.

Muay Thai has a basic stance that is similar to that of traditional boxing. However, boxing and Muay Thai have a major difference: in Muay Thai, kicking is more important than boxing. A Muay Thai fighter is prepared to kick at any time. The pressure on the heel is light. We start from the first position with two feet at shoulder width (1). Every person prefers a specific foot in front.

Note: someone who is right-handed should keep the left leg/foot in front. A left-handed person should stand with the right foot in front.

From the shoulder-width stance, the "stronger" foot has to turn 180 degrees (2). Leave the ball of the foot on the ground and turn the heel. All toes face front. Most fighters keep 50-60 cm between the feet. Try to keep this space at all times.

1

Basic stance,
shoulder width

2

First turn foot 180 degrees

When standing in this position, the pressure of the feet on the floor is mainly on the front part of the feet, which enables you to move lightly (3, 4).

Keep in mind that during training and fight you should keep a light touch on the ground, never let the heels set heavily on the ground, never put more weight on one leg or the other, always keep your knees a bit bent, and the hips in open position (5). The open position is easy to check – lift your knee (for a block or front kick); if you lose balance, your position is not good. Keep on trying it in every training session.

3

Move on front of foot and turn heel

4

Move left arm up to boxing position

5

Complete to final boxing position

We distinguish three different basic stance positions. We use the arm position as marker. Every fighter has his or her own position of the feet due to physical build and capabilities.

1. The original Muay Thai position with arms half bent. The open side of the fists are pointed toward the opponent. (6)
2. A position with the arms fully stretched and open palms directed at the opponent. (7)
3. The European position with a closed traditional boxing position, fists near the chin. (8)

6   7   8

Half way Muay Thai stance   *Long arm Muay Thai stance*   *Complete to final boxing position*

Position 1   The original Muay Thai position (see pictures 1-5)

This position depends on the gym and trainer. In general, we bring the total number of variations down to only two basic positions. During practice and fights, we use a combination of different positions. Daily practice develops a proper position and core stability. The feet are in position a little farther than shoulder width, around 50-60 cm apart from each other, and toes pointed toward the opponent.

To train this position to become automatic conditioning of the mind and body, use a piece of rope of 50-60 cm between your ankles (another way to measure the right size is to take a rope as long as the tip of your longest finger to the point of your elbow). Attach the rope between your ankles (do not forget to take an extra piece of rope as you need a string of rope around your ankles!) Another way to attach the rope is to use ankle belts as shown in the picture. When you move during the training session, the rope must stay stretched. This is the best way to learn to keep the feet apart from each other at all times.

When you use a mirror and, if possible, a video camera to check your movements, you are able to reach a higher control of performances. A variation to this stance can be done by bringing the weight closer to the leg in the back and by keeping the front leg free for front kicks.

The position of the arms is a 90-degree bend with the open side of the fists facing the opponent. The front fist is 50-60 cm away from the head at the height of the eyebrows, and the rear fist is 10-15 cm away from the cheeks. The fist in front is open and facing the opponent. The chin is firmly protected by pressing it against the chest and the inside of the shoulder of the front arm. The front part of the hip is moved a little upward to enable the chest to move up without opening the ribs to danger. This position is used because Thai fighters use more kick and knee actions. In this position, the hips are in a more open position. The open position allows easier walking in the ring when a person uses multiple kicks or knees.

Position 2   The specialist position (see picture 7)

The difference between position 1 and 2 is clearly visible in the position of the arms. In this position, the arms are nearly stretched. The elbows are slightly bent for fast grabbing. The hips are more open than in position 1. Position 2 is mainly used for people who are knee specialists. From this position, it is also easy to block kicks, grab the opponent and use the knees. Kicking from this position is a little more difficult than in other positions. Punching is also rather complicated but the use of elbows is very fast and easy.

This position is for the more advanced fighter as it is risky to perform. The defense system must be fast and complete. One very good thing about this stance is that traditional boxers hate it because fighters are grabbing them all the time to clinch and reduce distance so they can use the elbow and knee attacks.

Position 3   The European position (see picture 8)

This stance is mainly used by Western-style Muay Thai fighters. It is based on traditional boxing. The fists are closely placed next to the chin, elbows are closely against the side of the chest, and the arms are completely bent. The chin is protected by the fists and not pressed against the breast as in the former positions but slidely bent over. Be aware that this position is not exactly the same as the position in traditional boxing. A traditional Western boxer needs to have a firm stance on the feet and puts most of the weight on the front leg. This is not allowed in Muay Thai/kickboxing. You need to kick, use the knees or elbows, etc. You need to be light on your feet and able to block kicks with the shins. The body weight must balance between the two legs and be easily moved to the rear leg, knees always slightly bent and heels on the ground.

Position exercises

Stand in front of a mirror. Move to a basic position you want to train. For the first position, try to thrust a right knee without losing balance, and then return to the original position, step back and knee again, then repeat again. The next exercise is to step left and right. After each thrust, you have to return to a stable and controlled position.

A good training activity for Position 2 is the front kick with the left foot (if you are left-handed, use your right front leg). Start in stance 1 and move around without losing your balance. Position 3 is easier to train when combining punches and kicks. Training balance in 3 is a matter of balancing the upper and lower halves of the body. If you are a right-hander, stand with the left foot forward. First, you will give a left direct punch followed by a right and then a right round kick. Move around without losing your balance. Position 3 is called a moving balance position. Moving the balance over the body will result in time loss. This is a big disadvantage when fighting a Thai. Consider this when training.

11 WALKING AND SLIPPING

In all fighting arts, great attention is paid to the standing and moving positions. Balance is most important while moving. If you lose your balance, you are vulnerable to all actions of the opponent. In Muay Thai and ring sports in general, balance is the most essential. Losing your balance can result in a KO or a grounding (pinning). In this example activity, we assume the fighter is right-handed and has the left foot forward. We separate moving into four logical directions. It is important that while moving, regardless of the direction, the knees are a bit bent; never move with straight legs as that will always disturb your balance.

a)   Forward (see pictures 1-3)
b)   Backwards (see pictures 4-5)
c)   Left (see pictures 6-7)
d)   Right (see pictures 8-9)

a)   Walking and slipping forward (see pictures 1-3)
Going forward has different reasons for its use. If you have to follow the opponent over a longer distance, you need to "walk." When standing with the left foot in front, you move the right foot in front in a stepping movement without putting your full weight on the front leg. (Not shown in pictures here) When stepping, you must be ready at any given moment to block a low kick. "Walking" must be trained often.

Another way of moving forward over short distances is to step a little in front with the left foot (about 25-35 cm) (2). However, the balance is disturbed, and the distance between the left and right foot is too much. The right foot slides into the standard position (3) to regain balance again. During this fast movement, the weight shortly moves to the front leg.

b)   Moving backward (see pictures 4-5)
Going backwards is difficult without disturbing the balance. Most fighters avoid stepping back because they are not able to see where they are going, which is critical for a fighter. Most of the time, we step back with the right foot (4) and slide the left foot back to regain balance (5). When sliding back with the left foot, it is normal to place most of the weight on the right leg for a moment to be able to give a front kick or block a low kick while moving.

1

Basic fight stance

2

Move front leg forward

3

Pull back leg to balanced fight stance

4

Move back, first place back leg to the desired position

5

Pull front leg to fight stance

c)   Moving left (see pictures 6-7)

In a fight, we move around the opponent. In fact, moving around is dependent upon the basic stance of the fighter. In general, we know that a left foot in front implies a strong right kick or punch. When this is the case, you have to avoid this strong weapon by moving away from it. In this particular case, you move left while attacking. First, you move the left foot to the left (6) and regain balance by sliding the right foot back to the basic balance position (7). The movement must take place quickly as you place most of your weight on the left leg at the moment you slide the right leg into position.

6

*Move to the left, front foot
moves left first*

7

*Back leg moves to
fight stance*

8

*Move right, back leg moves
right first*

9

*Front leg follows to
fight position*

d)   Moving right (see pictures 8-9)

The right foot steps to the right side, (8) then slide the left foot into the balance position (9). Like stepping backwards, the weight will briefly be put on the right (back) leg so you are able to use the left for kicking or blocking.

In mixed martial arts, you find more wrestling-like stances. When trying to grab a person in a wrestling way, the position is usually low on the legs, and the back leg is deeply pressed into the floor to accelerate and move forward quickly when possible. The weight of the body is basically on the front leg, which makes this a dangerous position when facing low kicks.

Suggestion: A good way of training how to walk is to start in a fighting position and to train with front kicks while moving. For example, you start to give a front kick with the left foot. After the kick, the foot touches back on the ground and is immediately followed by a kick with the right foot. After this, you do not return the right foot to its old position but place it in front of the left foot in a new balance-perfect position. After this, you kick again with the left foot (which has to be moved from the back position to front), put the left in front again and kick with the right. Now you can train kicks, balance, and walking in one exercise.

12   FIST AND ARM TECHNIQUES

A clear overview of these techniques includes:

a)   Punches (direct hit, hook, and uppercut)
b)   Slamming (swing, back fist, uraken, swinging backfist)
c)   Elbow techniques

Punches

The Thai have different ways to punch. When they face traditional boxers, their defense is not strong enough. You can see this when they fight against Dutch, French, or English fighters, but you see it most clearly in Kadchuap fights. In Kadchuap, fighters have no gloves and most fights are held between Burmese boxers and Thai. Burmese are more specialized in punches than Thai. When fighting, you see that the Burmese try all efforts to hit the Thai in the face and are often successful. In the last 25 years, the Western style of boxing has been proven more effective in learning punches than any other style. One reason for this is that Western boxing training benefits from a regular input of scientific research for the development of speed, technical effort, conditioning, and special competitive performance. All is used to improve style and effectiveness in fighting and training.

Boxing is an art to be trained and practiced often; when exercised well it is possible to even use it as a fitness and health exercise in older age. Hitting is a combined action-reaction system. It is a play between targeting and pulling back. A slow hit has the effect of a brick on impact. A fast hit is like the sting of a bee (remember Muhammad Ali ?), it hurts!

Punches are divided into three categories:

*   direct (jabbing)
*   hook
*   uppercut

Direct punch (jabs) see pictures 1-8

Punching seems easy, but it is not. A punch is never made with the fist alone. A punch starts with an intuitive idea – an action set into motion. At nearly the same time the fist starts leaving the chin, at the same speed, the feet come into motion. The feet bring the power of the legs via the hips. The turn back is a linear force where the upper and lower bodies come into the same line of motion creating a maximum of speed and power. When working out, think of the power of the legs as 10x higher than the arm; it is important to use this power when punching.

A direct punch or jab starts from a basic balance position. Both fists are located next to the chin. To explain the punch, we divide the movement in parts. We start with the left straight punch.

1

1. The left foot steps in front (2).
2. The left fist leaves the chin in a straight line to the target (3).
3. During the move, the fist makes a quarter or 1/8 turn while the two main knuckles are directed at the target (4).
4. At the moment of impact, the right side of the body turns (you turn the left part of the hip to the right) and most of the body weight is brought behind the left punch (5).
5. The fist lands on the target with only two knuckles hitting the surface.
6. The right leg stretches in a way that its power is moved to the left fist.
7. Directly after impact, the fist is pulled back in a straight line to the chin while making a turn again in opposite direction (5-8).
8. With the right side the punch looks similar (9-12).

Total move: direct punch

2

3

4

Basic boxing stance in balance

Move toward the target

Move toward the target

5

Full stretched left jab

6

*Return to balanced
fighting position*

7

*Return to balanced
fighting position*

8

*Return to balanced
fighting position*

9

*Basic fight position
hands high*

10

Move toward target

11

Right straight jab

12

Pull back in straight line

13

Basic fight position

The left arm always has to stay slightly bent to avoid injury to the elbow. When a boxer has an elbow injury (in traditional boxing, it often happens), it implies that the boxer often missed his jabs or overstretched the arm. Either way, it will disable the boxer later in life. It is very important to be careful in training and competing because the elbow is a sensitive, small joint.

After impact, the left fist moves in a straight line back to the starting position. First, the fist moves back to the chin, the hips turn back into position and the feet start to react by moving left, or right, or front or backwards. To train this punch it is important to use a combination of standing in front of the mirror and critique all of your movements. Also, practice on a boxing bag to train for impact, and train workout coordination on the pads with a trainer or coach.

A right direct punch (jab) is made by moving the right fist in a straight line to the target. Just before impact, the hip starts to turn and reaches its maximum at moment of impact. The difference between right and left is that the hip must be turned deeper into the movement to bridge a bigger gap than the left. Moving back is done in a straight line exactly the same way it began. The right hip is drawn back in the same way as the movement of the left jab. By quickly twisting the hips, a fighter is easily able to let left and right follow each other.

Direct punches are made to several parts of the body such as head, plexus, and stomach. Punching in different areas changes the way of standing and moving, and most of all, demands a good manipulation of balance. The legs play a very important part in going up and down when punching and transferring the power of the body into the hits. Direct punches (jabs) must be trained very often. They are not only the bridge between you and the opponent, they also measure distance and teach you how to launch a punch, a knee, or a kick.

The fist of the punching arm is held in two positions. The first (training) position is with a full turned fist, and two knuckles are the hitting part (14). The other, faster way, is used in competition and has a slightly lighter turn. The elbow is not lifted as much as with the training punch (15).

14

You hit with these two knuckles of your fist

15

Half turn fist, fast punch

16

Left jab to plexus

17

Right jab to stomach

The jab is also placed on different parts of the body such as plexus (16) and stomach (17).

These punches are getting the right attention with the integration of Western boxing in Muay Thai now.

In partner and pad training the actions are more clear than in "shadow boxing." With a partner the movements are like in photos 18-19 and so on. For more professional use, it is trained on target pads and as shown in 20-21.

18

Working out with gloves

19

Downward right jab

20

Working with focus mitts

21

Left jab with focus mitts

Hook

A hook is launched from three different distances:

1. Long range, I call this 75% compared to the jab that is considered 100% (22)
2. 50%, or a 90-degree hook, the elbow is bent around a 90-degree corner (23)
3. 25%, or a short distance hook, this hook is between the uppercut and 50% hook (24).

22

23

24

Left hook 75%

Front view left hook 50% distance

Right hook 25% distance

25

Note: The crossover hook, can be placed at any of these three distances but crosses over the arm of the opponent (25).

Left blocks the hook by crossing over the hook in a counter attack

A long hook has one essential weak point – the wrist. Launching a long hook implies you wish to surpass the defense of the opponent and you have to bend the wrist a little. A hook is thrust "around the corner." When giving a direct punch (jab), we use a straight line (100%). A hook is given in a half-circle-like movement.

How is the hook launched (26)

26

Total move: hook

1. First, turn the body (if starting with a left hook) to the left side without letting the defense down. The turning point is in the hips. The fist leaves the chin in a circle-like movement in the direction of the opponent (27-34).
2. The fist is turned with the open side of the hand down to the ground (29).
3. The punch will hit the target with the two first knuckles (30).
4. At the moment the punch arrives at the target, the power of the hips/legs are behind it by using the maximum rotation.
5. To withdraw the fist, the movement starts by returning the hips to original position (31).
6. The fist moves back in a straight line to the same position, and the balance is re-established (32-33).

27

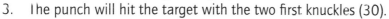

28

29

Basic fight position

30

31

32

Left hook 75% distance

33

34

Basic fighting position

Left hook 75% front view

Hooks are made with the hips as the center of the movement. To place a hook, you need to train the wrist when it is weak. It is very important to keep the wrist as stiff as possible at all times during punching, but it is the weakest point of the action.

A perfect training activity to strengthen the wrist is to fill a long-neck bottle with sand or water, then turn the bottle in circles and move it up and down.

A 50% hook has the elbow bent in a 90-degree angle. The basic movement is the same as that of a long hook. The difference is a rounder circle (35-36). To use maximum force, you have to turn the shoulder further into the movement. This also gives a better protection of your chin and head. When using a left hook at the moment of impact, the left leg will stretch to maximize power on impact. The return movement starts at the moment of impact in the legs by returning the left leg back to original position. The right hook follows the same directions but in the opposite direction. The difference is made in the legs because the right leg allows a higher impact most of the time as the length of the circle is so much bigger. A right-hander is usually more powerful in his right half. This power is due to the "swing" the right fist gets when turning the hip and leg for "throwing" the punch into the target.

In close combat situations, we can use a short hook. This kind of hook is made with a short, sharp turning of the hip and is not as powerful as the other hooks. But when the contact is made on the tip of the chin or the temples, the effects are realistic and a KO is often the result. Most of the time, the elbow cannot be lifted as high as other hooks, so this hook moves between an uppercut and a halfway hook. A right hook in close combat often follows a little bigger circle than the left and lands on the backside of the chin part. Sometimes it lands on the back of the head (37).

35

36

Left hook on the pads

A crossover hook is made as a counter-defense attack. When the opponent is hitting with a direct jab, the jab is blocked by one hand and, by the other hand, a hook is placed over the hitting arm (38).

In Muay Thai or ring sports other than boxing, hooks are mainly aimed at the head, especially by beginning fighters and during sparring. Hooks to other parts of the body, such as the liver and spleen, are only made by the real masters of the art. A very good example is Rob Kaman, who grounded a few of his opponents by a perfect hook to the liver followed by low kick. A good hook to the liver is always a good follow-up

37

Total move: crossover hook

38

Right crosses over with a left counter hook

hit. A liver punch is a danger to your thumb it is advised to always mind your thumb! Often fighters hit the elbow of the opponent and injure the hand. An injury on the thumb is hard to heal. It is advised to always wear gloves with a good thumb protection and, if possible, one in which the thumb is attached to the rest of the glove. When injured, use strong wrapping to hold the thumb more closely to the hand and avoid relaxing it. Your fist needs to be a real fist in these situations.

The Liver Punch (39)

The fist leaves the chin and makes a circular movement in the direction of the liver of the opponent. At the same time, the body is bent over a little to the left side and the left leg is also bent a little to decrease height. Bridging distance and height is important during this movement. Defense of the right side of the body is important at the moment you make this move. The right side of the chin must be carefully protected by your right fist. To improve power into the punch, it is best to move the hip and leg behind the arm as a "back-up" power system (40-46). The return of the fist, again, must follow a straight line directly to the chin. A right hook to the spleen is often trained but seldom used as it is not very effective in a fighting situation. It moves the same way as the left liver hook but in the opposite direction.

39

Total move: liver punch

40

41

42

Basic fighting position

Liver punch left

43

44

45

Liver punch front view

46

Partner training liver punch

Other body punches are made to the floating ribs (eleventh and twelfth ribs) and the solar plexus (47-51).

47

Partner training spleen punch

48

Pad training spleen punch

49

Right punch to stomach

50

Downward right jab

51

Right jab to stomach

Uppercut (52)

Uppercuts are very effective but rarely used weapons in any fight. There are two places of the body that are targets: the head and the plexus or stomach area. Just as when launching a hook, the uppercut movement is circular. The difference is that a hook circles to the side of the body and an uppercut goes to the front of the body. We can distinguish the same three distances as we did with the hook. Uppercuts are made in a wave-like movement. These hits are rarely made as single blows. The wave-like movement comes from the legs and "bobbing and weaving."

The fist leaves the chin in a circular movement in the direction of the target. This time, the circle is made in the direction of the opponent's body directly, unlike the hook that moves around "a corner." Depending on the distance, the arm is bent in a different angle.

- A long uppercut has an arm bent in a 90-degree angle (53). The fist can be held in two different positions:
  a) open hand part facing toward your own face; or b) the thumb facing your own face. Option B is a way for the uppercut to slip through someone's defense. It is not as powerful as the normal uppercut (hand opening, facing your own face) but it can shock the opponent for a moment and create openings for further actions. The power of the uppercut comes mainly from the legs. At the moment of impact, the legs stretch and impact is maximized. It is immediately followed by bending the knees again and pulling back the fist.

52

Total move: uppercut

- A halfway uppercut (54-60) is made the same way as a long distance one. The difference is the impact of the uppercut. A halfway is much harder, faster and more difficult to avoid. The elbow angle is around 90 degrees, the open side of the fist is toward you, and the hitting edge is again the two front knuckles. The power is generated from the hips and legs by supporting the upward movement of the punch. Look at the pictures and try to make the same movement often. Uppercuts are always made in combination with other punches.

Body uppercuts are made in close combat situations and in series. In Muay Thai, you seldom will see them made because the head is not protected enough and it is very likely to receive elbow blows. In other ring fights, for instance in a ground situation, the body blows are very useful. Training these hits is best practiced in front of a mirror, with a partner or with pads.

53

Long uppercut with pads

54

Partner training uppercut

55

Basic fighting position

56

57

Uppercut with the left, 90 degree turned, fist

58

59

Pull back in straight line, basic position

60

Front view, look at the position of elbow

Uppercuts are forgotten weapons in most fights. The main reason is that during training people pay to less attention to the way the body must support the uppercut to be powerful. An uppercut is, like all other punches, very much dependent upon stability and core balance. If the body leans out of position, the punch will not land at the targeted spot. Uppercuts are also combination punches; they must be trained in combination with other punches to be effective and enjoyable in training situations. It is very important that you avoid using only the shoulder so that you prevent injuries!

Hitting the right way

Whatever punch you make, you must have a good basic technique in using the knuckles and keeping the wrist in the right position. Picture 61 shows how to use only two knuckles for all punches. It is important to use them in the right way and support the power by keeping the wrist straight and strong. We have outlined three phases during the punch:

You hit with these two knuckles of your fist

1. Relaxation phase: the fists are near the head and the muscle tension is as low as possible.
2. Preparation phase: the eyes preceive the possibility to hit. The brain sends impulses to the muscles for activation, and the muscles are stimulated by the nerves to start an action. The fist is not yet fully tensed and not completely closed.
3. Impact phase: the fist lands on the target and is fully tensed. All muscles are in full contraction and the fist is completely closed.

After this last phase, we distinguish between the opposites in tension and relaxation in the muscular and neural systems. In this action, we clearly see that boxing is a game of coordination and uses impulses to and from the brain. We call this hand-eye coordination, which is a very important system to train the reflexes of the body and mind.

A way to train the use of the two knuckle system is by doing push-ups on the two knuckles. The best way to train this is to use a solid surface and really feel the knuckles press. In this exercise, you must focus on the right stance of the knuckles and fist and not on the push-up part of the activity.

Another very important part of hitting is the position of the wrist. I have followed many different boxing trainers and coaches. Each has his or her own vision of how to hold the wrist straight. In this book, I promote safety before ideology and stick to the medical opinion of the best way to keep a wrist safe from injury. In my opinion, the wrist needs to be "stiff"; it is not allowed to bend during the moment of impact.

A short, scientific explanation is that impact power is a combination of two different forces. One force is made by the person who gives the punch. The other force is given by the receiver. A receiver is not a passive object, he/she is moving all the time to avoid being hit. By moving, the power that is produced returns a force during the moment of impact of a punch. Compare it with two cars in an accident. Both add a force to the collision causing damage to both vehicles, even at low speed. When the wrist is bent, even a little, the power carries via a straight line principle back into the wrist. Because of the straight line, the impact power follows any angle that disturbs this line and receives a maximum power pressure on that point. If the point is weak enough, an injury is created. This accounts for any angle, even the slightest. I call this the principle of the vector of power. It is easy to prove.

For safety, I think it is important we address "wrapping" the hands. Hand wraps are widely used in most contact sports to prevent injuries to the wrist or hand. A hand wrap has two functions:

1. To protect the hand from being injured
2. To soak up the sweat from the activity

We can distinguish two kinds of hand wraps, which in turn can be made into many variations:

1. Training wrap
2. Competition wrap

A wrap is a piece of bandage with a length of between 2.5 and 5 meters. It is made from cotton with an elastic component to make it easier to wrap around the hand. The width of the wrap is a maximum of 4 cm. On one end of the wrap, we have a dumb lock and the other end a Velcro closure.

The training wrap is made by placing the wrap around the hand without going between the fingers (62-70). It is a simple and fast way to wrap the hand.

62

First step, put the tape around your thumb

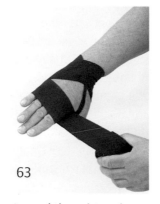

63

Around the wrist and to the hand

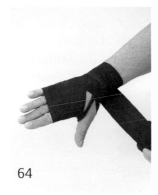

64

Wrap few times around hand in overlapping order

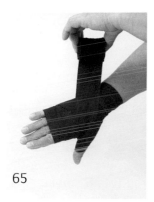

65

Turn the wrap around the thumb to lock it in

66

Wrap around hand

67

Wrap over the wrist in a fish bone pattern

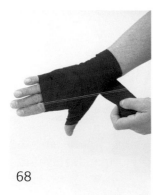

68

End at the wrist

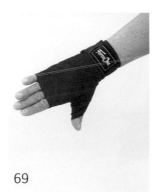

69

Final wrap; do you see the fish bone wrap?

70

The fist ready to hit

A competition wrap takes the wrap between the fingers and follows a special bone supporting pattern where we also see the vector principle. When you put the wrap between the fingers, the bone structures in the hand come apart a little. Upon hitting, you apply a force to the bones in a not-so-natural way. Although it is only a fraction of a millimeter, this little change in power direction is able to damage the bone eventually. In my daily practice, I have treated many boxers with fist injuries and one of the most common problems is due to the wrapping.

Do we always need to wrap our hands for boxing?

This question has been asked of me many times. The answer is, no, you do not need to wrap. But this answer is immediately followed by the fact that wrapping is better for most people because it supports the wrist and forces the hand into a good boxing position. Also, it is important as a sweat absorber to protect the gloves from becoming soaking wet.

Series and combinations (71-77)

Boxing techniques are trained in combinations. In this book, I illustrate a few combinations. During training, many more combinations are thought by you. It is important to keep in mind that the training of series must be logical. In a real fight, the fighter is hardly ever able to give more than 3 to 4 punches before the opponent escapes or starts the counter. Training of more than 6 to 8 combination punches is useless and will not improve your abilities. For most fighters, a series of more than 5 punches is already hard to memorize, let alone more than 6.

Training combinations of punches with a partner increases abilities, reflexes, and flexibility. When practicing, stick to certain rules:

- Always keep the fists near the chin.
- Punch and return always in a straight line (the shortest possible).
- Every movement starts from the legs.
- Your basic stance must be in balance and enable you to move easy and swiftly.
- Practice "walking" in the ring every day or in front of a mirror.
- Never use only one punch when training; combinations enable you to learn the body better to respond to opponents and train to keep moving whatever the situation.
- Play your own game, never lose control (e.g., become angry), stay alert and do not copy or let someone force a strategy upon you.

71

Left jab

72

Right jab

73

Left hook

74

Right uppercut

75

Left hook

76

Right jab

77

Left liver punch

Other methods to hit

In Dutch/Western Muay Thai some moves from karate/Taekwondo are incorporated. If we look back at ancient Muay Thai (before the '30s), we find all these movements as a part of the traditional fighter's technical arsenal in combat. For the sake of Western knowledge and recognition, I will use the more common names (not the Thai).

A strike is a movement made with the fist or an open hand. The point of contact with the opponent is on the side of the hand or the backside. Examples of these movements are:

- Swing (78)
- Backfist (82-84)
- Swinging backfist (85-88)
- Uraken (90-93)
- Other karate-like open hand hits (94-97)

Most mentioned strikes are no longer used in Muay Thai or kickboxing fights but are common in free fights and other ring sports. Most of the time, they are on the prohibited movement lists. In boxing, sometimes competing opponents use the side of the hand on areas where the entering of the big glove is not possible. Of course, those techniques are not allowed.

For real kickboxing and sometimes Muay Thai or Kachuab a (swinging) back fist or uraken can be very useful. But the real Muay Thai/Kachuab fighter is very cautious in using them as they will expose the back. A swing is used in all fights.

Swing (79-81)

The swing is a circular hit with the backside knuckle part of the fist. Traditional boxing has banned it. The movement is rather simple. The fist is turned away from the chin and starts a circular movement toward the opponent. The power in this movement is created by the full body weight and turning of the hips. The hips will turn 180 degrees. The movement can be considered a "throwing" of the fist toward the opponent. The risk of the movement lies in the withdrawal of the fist. When the opponent successfully defends against this hit, it is easy to penetrate your defense and attack with full power.

78

Swinging left fist hits with backside of the fist

79

Sudden hand drop

80

Fist turns with back of hand to partner

81

Hit with backside of the knuckles of the fist

Backfist (82-84)

This hit is often made after missing a hook or other punch, and you no longer are in a complete balance. For instance, you launch a hook toward the head of your opponent, but he ducks and then comes up again. Your fist has passed his head and you are not able to hit with the front part of the knuckles again. In fact, the backside of the fist is now pointing in the direction of the opponent's head. By turning the hips in the opposite direction and using the backside of the hand as a weapon, you "throw" back the fist.

82

Start back fist, often after a missed hook, right hand

83

Fist moves back, turn back of hand to partner

84

Hit with back side of the fist

Swinging backfist (85-88)

This swinging hit is made when turning around your center point. A better name is "spinning backfist." The movement is made by turning the whole body around its center without losing balance (keeping your balance is the most difficult part). Train as follows: make a left hook in the air, do not stop the movement but keep going; and step to the right with the left foot following the left hook. After this, you start to turn the shoulders and the right arm comes into action. At the moment the right fist leaves the chin, the right foot steps out. The backside of the right hand lands on the side of the opponent's head.

85

Basic training position

86

Start of turn for right hand hit

87

Always look before you hit

88

Sweeping hit with back of hand after turning the body

Uraken

This is a typical karate move, often seen among Japanese fighters. It is a point move and not effective to reach a KO. The fist is in its normal position with the opening toward your own face. The knuckle part now moves in a straight line toward the opponent. When the arm is nearly stretched, the return movement begins. You can compare the movement with that of a wipe.

90

Basic set right hand hammer fist possible after a hook block

91

Right hammer fist

92

93

Other karate-like open hand hits

Hit with palm=inside of the hand

Fist turns with back of hand to partner

Hit with backside of the knuckles of the fist

Defense and bobbing and weaving

Defending oneself is most important when fighting. Every received punch is not only an unwelcome present but also leaves some damage. It is better to defend yourself!

We can define defense as blocks and evading (bobbing and weaving). In Muay Thai or kickboxing, sometimes defending is not easy to do. To begin, I will explain the defense as used in traditional boxing and identify the useful differences when fighting in the ring using Muay Thai or kickboxing.

Defense on a straight punch (98-100)

From the basic stance (left foot front), the opponent throws a left straight at you. There are two ways to block this punch. First, using the left hand, move it to the right to push away the coming punch. The negative side of this movement is that your defense of the left side of the head becomes weak. A right punch can follow and surely will reach its target. Instead, using the right hand to block the left hand will make the return movement of the opponent more difficult. When using the right hand for defense, you give way for cross punching.

When receiving a right punch, the best way to block is using the left hand. When the punch comes at you, move the punch to the (right) side.

Alternative ways to block are to push the coming punch down (best used when you are taller than the opponent) or pushing it up (when you are shorter than the opponent).

98

Basic training position

99

Left blocks the left jab with the right hand then moves inward

100

Left arm block

Defending against a hook (101-103)

Defending against a hook is a matter of closing down the defense of the body with both arms. By creating tension in the muscles, you are able to block a direct hit but remember that you will always be confronted with the energy of the punch and will receive the power through your body. Protecting the head is easier when you make yourself smaller by pressing the chin down on the chest, bending the arm, bringing the glove against the head and increasing to maximum tension.

Hooks to the body are blocked with the arms. Do not forget to put the arms close to the body; leave no space, otherwise you'll be knocked down by your own elbow.

101

Basic training position

102

Left blocks a left hook with right arm

103

Right gives a right hook, left blocks with left arm

104

Left blocks a left liver punch with his elbow

Defending body punches (104)

Keeping a good elbow near body position is the best defense against body punches.

Bobbing and weaving

This technique is called like this because your body moves up and down like a wave of the sea. On a straight punch, the head moves to the side. It strongly depends on which position the body holds as to which side you choose at that particular moment.

We train to move to the right when receiving a left jab and to the left when receiving a right jab. When moving to the side we use our "pushing defense" to provide extra protection. This is called cross punching.

On hooks, we react by moving down. When a hook is launched to the head, you bend the knees and go down in a circular movement. First, your head follows the direction of the punch and then, when down, you move back in the same circular movement. In fact, you go around in circles.

Real Muay Thai fighters are wary of bobbing and weaving due to the use of the knees. When a head goes down, a fighter's reaction is to throw a knee toward the head. If the knee hits the head, it will leave some kind of damage.

Uppercut defense (105-107)

To defend yourself against an uppercut is not easy. The only possible way is to lower one of your hands in the direction of the coming uppercut. This way your power goes against the hit and neutralizes it.

105

Basic training position

106

Left blocks a right uppercut with right hand

107

Left blocks a left uppercut with left hand

Elbow techniques

The elbow is one of the most dangerous weapons in fighting arts. Nothing covers the rock-hard bone structure and every blow is devastating to the opponent. The art of using the elbow has been best developed by the Thai. In many countries, the elbow blow is prohibited due to its extreme power and effect when it hits the neck, head, or spine. In self-defense courses, the power of the elbow is underestimated, and I strongly advise specialists to add this weapon to defense trainings!

Elbow techniques can be categorized as follows:

*   The most commonly used elbow technique is the one that comes from the side like a hook; we call it the roundhouse elbow (108).
*   A lesser used technique is the uppercut elbow (109).
*   A technique that is barely used is the elbow that comes from over the head and down; we call it "down to earth" (110).

- The back swing elbow comes from a 180-degree turn of the body (111).
- A pushing elbow is moved from the body. It is not possible to put enough power in this elbow hit to knock someone down (112).

108

Right swing elbow to the head

109

Straight rising elbow directly on target

110

111

Turning the body and prepare right backward elbow

112

Elbow to the stomach

Roundhouse elbow (see pictures 113-120)

When making a hook, put the elbow behind the fist and back up the fist with the full power of the body. While giving a roundhouse elbow, the fist does not leave the original position. Instead, the elbow moves in the direction a hook does. When the target is reached, begin to pull back at the moment of impact.

In Muay Thai, we have a combination of elbows in which the roundhouse elbow plays an role. When fighting and missing the first elbow, the body is turned 180 degrees and the target is hit with the other elbow from the backside. At the moment of impact, your back is turned toward the opponent. The movement must be made quickly to avoid allowing your opponent a chance to hit your back (see pictures).

113

Basic fighting position

114

The elbow is lifted while still protecting the head

115

The right elbow hits the target

116

Basic fight stance

117

Turn in the right elbow to hit

118

Right elbow hits the target

119

Return to basic position

120

Right swing elbow to the head

Uppercut elbow (121-123)

An uppercut elbow comes from a low position and goes in straight line from the chin. The movement starts from a boxing position with the elbows at the sides of the body. The fist could be held in two different ways: one (for instance when giving a right elbow) next to the left ear (a crossed elbow) or next to the right ear. The power development is like the uppercut from the lower part of the body. After impact, the elbow moves back to exactly the same position at the sides while preparing the rest of the body for other actions.

121

Basic fighting position

122

Start of straight rising elbow right

123

Final position straight rising elbow (look at hand position)

A cross variation on this technique is seen in pictures 124-127 as the fist goes down over the opposite shoulder.

124

Basic fighting position

125

Left cross rising elbow, look at hand position

126

Final position at moment of impact

127

Down to earth elbow (110)

The direction of this elbow is from above the target in the direction of the ground. The elbow can be used in two ways. One way it can be used is to jump up and lift the elbow over the shoulder to let it come down on the target. Another way is to pull or push the opponent down and then launch the elbow at the intended target.

Back swing elbow

The back swing elbow is often made when a boxing or other elbow technique missed target. It is the most effective self defense method as the opponent is not able to see the action coming (128-131). A variation on this in 132-134. All of these are extremely effective and mainly used in close combat situation.

Elbows are always used in combinations with other techniques to be more effective. In fighting, the elbow and knee are often used together. In Muay Thai, the elbow is used in combination with boxing techniques. Because Thai box in a different way than Europeans do, the effectiveness of the elbow must be trained accordingly.

The elbow is a very practical weapon when used in self-defense. It is the bone structure that is harder than a fist and less sensitive.

Basic training position

Attack with left straight elbow

Do not pull back to original position but continue

Turning the body and prepare right backward elbow

132

Basic training position

133

Turn back to the partner but keep looking

134

Turn with a direct low elbow to the
abdomen

13 KICKING TECHNIQUES

Kicks are made with different parts of the leg. The most important body part in full contact martial arts is the upper part of the shin. The bone (tibia) is strong and thick. Other kicks are made with the instep, heel, ball, or side of the foot.

1

Total move: Turn kick

Front kick, look at arm position

2

Kicks are categorized as follows:

* **roundhouse kicks (1)**
* **straight kicks (also called front kick) (2)**
* **side kicks (3)**
* **special, sweep-like kicks (4)**
* **turning kicks (5)**
* **back kicks (6)**

3

Side kick performed

4

Front kick in face

Turning side kick with left leg   *Prepare leg for heel kick*

Before we continue, I would like to explain the difference between the Thai way of kicking and the Western way. Thai kicks do not just lift the leg off the ground and kick the target. Kicking is a movement of harmony between body and mind – a movement that needs to be perfected and trained accordingly. Kicks need to be trained by repetition. In Muay Thai camps, the same movement is trained on a daily basis for a number of years showing that practice makes perfect.

There are many different ways to train kicks:

- with a partner (always under guidance of a qualified trainer/teacher)
- on striking pads (see pictures)
- on the boxing bag

In martial arts, we have many different directions and interpretations concerning how to kick. Japanese and Korean fighters prefer to kick with the forefoot/instep and not the shin. Thai prefer to kick with the shin. Each method has its pros and cons, and your preference depends upon your personal style practice.

It is a fact that the instep/forefoot is weaker than the shin. When you kick, the impact of the shinbone on the body is harder than that of the instep/forefoot. But when you want to kick at higher levels, such as the head, the shin is not typically a practical weapon. If you wish to reach the head with a shin kick, you must be very flexible.

It is advised to train all techniques that can be used in actual fighting when you wish to go into a full contact battle. The wider your arsenal, the more chances you have. But, having a lot of techniques available will not always give you the upperhand. In full contact fighting, routine or better programming of the body is one of the most important parts of training. Each technique or combination must be trained thousands of times to make the actions more like reflexes instead of needing to think of what to do when in action. Thoughts are always slower than reflexes.

Roundhouse Kick

Roundhouse kicks are made at different heights. A typical Muay Thai kick is the "low kick." A low kick is made on both sides of the leg; one to the inside and one on the outside of the leg. The exact place to kick is around 5-7 cm above the knee. The nerves located in that area are very sensitive for an outside low kick. The low kick is the trademark of the Dutch fighters.

7

Basic fighting position

8

Preparation of inside low kick

9

Low kick on inside of leg

Low kicks made to the inside (7-9) of the thigh are used to disturb an opponent's balance. It is not possible to kick with the middle part of the shin as the foot will hit the other leg of the opponent. The kick is executed with the under part of the shin or sometimes with the instep!

The inside low kick is executed from every position. When training with a partner or on the bag, always concentrate on your own balance when kicking and returning the leg to the original position. When kicked on the nerve center as located in the central part of the inner thigh, the opponent may lose complete control over the leg.

Low kicks made with the shin to the outside (10-16) of the thigh are very efficient. To make one on the left leg (the opponent stands with his left leg front), you step to the left side with the left foot (at an angle of 45 degrees), then your position is like a bow and arrow for the right leg. The tension on the kicking leg increases in power.

Basic training position

Preparation for a low kick

Low kick on the leg, look at place for kicking

Training roundhouse kick on striking pad

14

Preparation of high rise or low kick

15

Lifting leg as high as possible

16

Drop low kick down on stricking pad

Kicking the front leg is rather easy. It is more complicated to kick the back leg correctly. To kick the leg that stands at the back when the left leg is in front position, move around the defense of the front leg and create an opening to kick safely.

The kick that is often used is the one to the liver, kidneys, and spleen (17). The difference between a low kick and a midsection kick is not only the height but the total movement. Kicks with the right leg: Starting from a basic position (left foot front), open the position by stepping to the left. The "bow and arrow" position creates a maximum tension for the kick. When the right leg leaves the ground to kick, the arms move in a different position. The left arm goes on top of the head to protect and the right arm moves back to counterbalance the moving kick. Even at the moment of impact, the knee stays bent a little to absorb the power of impact and protect the knee against injury. Before you start to kick, the end focus of the kick must not be the object that you wish to kick but at least half a meter

17

Blocking a kick on the legs

behind that point! To create high power in the kick, you need to focus on a point past the impact point. You must imagine kicking right through the target. When you miss the target, a perfect circular movement brings you back to the original starting position.

On impact of the target, the return movement starts with a "bouncing back." When a target is not made of wood or stone, when you hit it, the object projects a "bounce back." At the moment your leg gets the "bounce back," the leg moves back to the original position. The standing foot turns back on the ball of the foot like when moving toward the object. The right arm swings back to a frontal position and the left arm returns to its lower position. At the moment the right foot hits the ground, the whole body is back to the original position.

In Muay Thai, there was a time that most fighters turned around from a standard left foot in front to a right foot in front in the fighting position. The fighters specialized in left leg kicks. If a fighter kicks with his front leg, that is the leg which are in front in the basic fighting position, the power in the kick is lower than if kicked with the leg from the back position. In the beginning it was an advantage over opponents but soon all fighters turned over and the advantage was neutralized.

Executing a roundhouse kick to the body with the front (left) leg is a combination of several seemingly wider movements. To kick at different heights, the hips need to be "open." To open the hip, the heel of the right foot must not be on the ground and balance is moved to the front part of the body. A left kick is always made when moving. The best way to get maximum power is to step a little to the right with the right foot (see drawing). The left leg is powered by creating a bow & arrow stance. When the left leg leaves the ground, the knee points in the direction that the shin is expected to land on the opponent's body. A kick is launched while focusing not on the target but far behind it. You must have the will to kick through the object and not on it. When kicking, the arms play an opposite and balance controlling role. The power of the kick goes in one direction, and the arms will counteract to create a balance

(18-19). At the moment of impact, the return begins. Pulling back starts in the bouncing and turning back of the hip. The arms return to their original position. When the foot touches the ground, immediately start to move the whole body away/around.

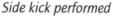

Side kick performed

Drop low kick on striking pad

A variation in the body kick is the blocking or stopping kick. This kick is turned in so far that the shin is completely over the stomach of the opponent. It is not possible to kick at that moment, but you will be able to use a push, using mainly the knee side of the shin to push away the opponent. A way to train the "kick" is to wait until a swinging boxing bag comes toward you and, at that moment, kick. The bag must come to a complete standstill at the moment of impact.

Kicks in the neck and head are mainly made with the lower part of the shin near the ankle and the foot. These kicks must be speedy and flexible. Thanks to the Thai climate, the muscles and joints of Thai fighters are flexible. In colder climates, you have to do stretching and flexing exercises to reach the same quality in kicking.

A practical training of kicking to the midsection or high areas is the same. The difference is found in the way to "open" the hips and let the leg turn around in the pelvic bone and balance with the upper body.

To train fast high kicks, try these suggestions:

- Put a tennis ball on an elastic rope and hang it on the ceiling at head level. Then kick the ball once and try to do it again while it is moving.
- The Thai sport sepak takraw is known as volleyball played only with the feet. The game is to keep a rattan ball as high as possible while kicking it over a net. Kicking it strengthens the legs and at the same time creates more flexibility. The "service," or serving the ball by kicking it over the net to the other side requires a lot of flexibility and precision. When you "serve," you need to kick the ball hard and fast to the other side. To do this, you need to be fast and kick high. In defense against attacks by the opponent, it is very important to have fast reflexes and high kicks.

A kick in the neck is given by the lowest part of the shin. As a target point, choose the place between the cheek and the spine just under the ear. This is a "deadly blow" and nearly always results in a KO. Records prove that some professional Thai fighters have lost their lives due to this kick. In history, some "super fights" are mentioned between Thai and Burmese where the Thai killed the opponent with this kick.

To make this kick with the front leg demands a good walking technique. It is very important that the heel of the standing leg is on the ground. When moving forward, the angle toward the opponent needs to be 45 degrees. When the foot of the kicking leg leaves the ground, the hip has to turn the front of the shin, which must "face" the target. At the moment of impact, the hip receives an extra turn spurred by the upper body and arms. When you hit the target (for instance striking pads), the return is initiated in the hips and guided down in a combination of arms/upper body/footwork. The best way to train this kick is to kick twice in a row. Doing this will help you learn to turn and move the feet, hips, arms, and leg in the right form.

Front kick (20-23)

You can compare the front kick with a jab in boxing. A good fighter often uses this front directed kick. With this kick, you keep distance between yourself and the opponent but also can attack or use it purely as defense.

20

Basic training position

21

Start of kick, pointing
knee in direction

22

Front kick, look at arm
positions

23

Return to position

To do this kick, start to lift up your knee to the height of the target position without losing balance. The foot moves in a straight line toward the direction of the opponent. At the moment of impact, the upper part of the body moves backward to support the power of the kick, with the arms in the same position as they are in all other kicks. The arms make the defense movements where one arm protects the head and the other is used as counterweight. After the target is hit, the withdrawal of the leg is in a straight line and mirrors the same path as making the kick. The natural law that "a straight line is the fastest way to the target" is also applicable here. Efficient fighting means keeping the way to the target as short as possible and to waste as little energy as possible.

Kick with the foot. From the foot, you may use different body parts. A typical karate kick is made with the ball (the part just under the toes) of the foot. It is possible to also use the heel and the flat foot.

When you learn to kick with the front leg, you get to know the kick with the leg that stands in the back. This is more difficult. For instance, when kicking with the right leg, it has to move over a long distance and is not as effective as a defense kick. But the attack kick is very useful.

Side Kick and Spinning Side Kick

This kick is hardly used by Thai when fighting because your back has less protection. Originally, this kick was used in Taekwondo and karate. A side kick is, as the word suggests, made sideways. In a ring sport like Muay Thai, this kick is considered dangerous because when the target is missed, the back is exposed to the opponent. If the opponent's reaction is a kick to your unprotected back, there is the possibility the spine could be hurt.

The effectiveness of the side kick has been proven numerous times. It became widely known by Bruce Lee who used it in all his movies. In ring fights, a well-known user was Benny "the Jet" Urquidez, who made the spinning side kick into an art form and his trademark.

To perform the kick, follow these steps:

1. Turn the side of your body to your opponent.
2. Lift the leg sideways and bend the upper body in the opposite direction (when training, use a chair to support your balance) (24).
3. The height of the knee is the height where the kick will be launched. The foot is bent and the "knife side" of the kicking foot is directed toward the opponent (25).
4. The foot leaves in a straight line. Upon impact, an extra push is given by the hip and the backward-moving upper body (26-27).
5. After impact, the foot moves back in a straight line back to the starting position.
6. Return to original fighting position by moving the hips back and put the feet firmly back on the ground.
7. Do not forget to control your hands at all times as they are your first line of defense.

24

Prepare leg for heel kick

25

Complete heel kick

26

Prepare for kick

27

Side kick left leg

A spinning side kick is executed differently:

1. Stand in a basic fighting position; left foot front and hands in boxing position.
2. Measure the distance between you and your opponent.
3. When you plan to kick with the right foot, the left foot moves to the right side in a 45-degree angle, toes pointing to the right, heel off the ground (28-29).
4. The left arm makes a circular movement to the right, and the right arm makes a backward (elbow) movement to the left (30-31).
5. The right leg moves up and the knee starts to point in the kick direction (32).
6. When moved to kicking position, the foot leaves the body and is launched in the side of the opponent's body. The target is the liver.
7. The start of the return is the returning of the arms to their original position.
8. The legs follow and return to fighting position.

28

Turn back for back kick

29

Back kick

Prepare for heel kick

Open the hip

Complete heel kick

This is a very powerful kick but when you miss, it easily can bring damage upon you. If you really want to use it, you must practice it daily. Restoring balance after the kick is difficult due to the circular movement. The best way to practice is against a body shield or a moving bag/object. This kick is becoming popular again in mixed martial art fights and related tournaments. The kick is spectacular for spectators.

Heel Kick (33-35)

A heel kick from the standing position is basically used in Japanese, Indonesian, and Korean martial arts. Western fighters have introduced this kick in the ring. In K1, it has proven to be effective and has scored different KOs.

33

Basic training position

34

Turning around to prepare for kick

35

Complete turn and prepare to kick

36

When you kick with the heel, you expose the back completely to the opponent. We use a kick with the right heel as an example. To kick with the right heel, I have to step in front of the right foot to come into kicking position. In this move, I expose my back as little as possible to my opponent. But moving this way, I block the possible kicks of my left leg.

When the kick starts, the heel moves in a straight line to the head of the opponent. During the move up, the upper body moves downward to open the hips. The moment the heel reaches the height of the head, the knee bends and the kick lands on the head. To return to the original position, go back the same way as you came. A Taekwondo fighter is very capable of doing this kind of kick more than

once. I have met fighters in kukkiwon (Korea) who could stand on one leg and continuously kick with the other leg. It is magnificent to watch, but in full contact fights it is not very useful.

The effectiveness of the kick is a different issue for the turning heel kick. The power of this kick is something to be accounted for. In Taekwondo, I learned a perfect combination of a roundhouse kick followed by a spinning/turning heel kick. Of course, it is possible to use the technique as an independent kick, but the hidden power is clearly visible.

For training purposes, this is how to execute an independent kick.

Begin in the basic stance, left foot front, right at shoulder width behind. Start the movement when you step to the right with the left foot. The left foot passes the right leg for at least 50 cm before touching the ground again. When beginning to step, the feeling on the right side is to turn into a circular movement. The right arm is used as a catalyst to start the movement of the right foot upward. The right heel has to go in the circular movement directly toward the target. The knee is a bit bent. Keeping the knee a bit bent will protect it from overstretching at the moment of full impact.

The best way to practice the kick is against a boxing bag. When training on a striking pad (big shield to be hold by your partner, see equipment section), the partner is not allowed to move when the kick is made. From my own experience, things can go very wrong when the partner moves away. I tore all the ligaments in my knee due to the sudden movement of the person who was holding my striking pad.

A point to note with all turning motion kicks is the sudden loss of balance, especially if you miss the target. The only way to learn to restore your balance is to control the movement in combination with a beginning or follow-up technique.

Back-kick or donkey kick

When the opponent is able to come behind you there is one kick that can protect you from the attack. This kick is mainly done with the heel. First, lift the knee, then bend the body a bit to create tension in the muscles and then eject the leg at full power.

Special Kicking Techniques (37-44)

These techniques are not often used but are nice to learn, especially when you are in an over-class position. To be in an over-class position in a fight is to be far superior in skill to your opponent.

A nice technique is the wipe kick. You kick the opponent with the instep of the foot on the side of the face. We start in left foot for position. Lift the knee to chest height and sweep the left foot like a wipe to the left side of the face. On impact, pull back, which creates a sweeping effect. You can apply this also with the right foot.

Basic training position

Axe kick to head or collar bone

Axe kick on striking pad

Landing of axe kick in full power

There is also a kick often seen in Taekwondo and introduced in the ring by Korean and Brazilian fighters. It is made by a circular movement. Start in the basic position, left foot forward. Now use the right leg. Lift the knee to the height and point it in the direction you wish to kick. Then the foot moves toward the face of the opponent. Upon impact, push a little more before pulling back (37-40).

A dropping heel kick is borrowed from Taekwondo. It is sometimes called the axe kick because it comes down like an axe on the head. For tall fighters, this technique is great for destroying the opponent's confidence. It is also very effective. Start with the left foot front position. The knee goes up in a circular movement to its highest possible position. At the highest position, the under part of the leg moves up fast. At the moment the leg is stretched and positioned over the opponent's head, the heel moves down! The target you should hit is the top, center of the head, where the fontanelles come together.

When this kick effectively lands on the head or shoulder, you will be surprised by its devastating effect! A negative side effect of the kick is a complete loss of balance when the opponent knows how to block and counter the kick.

Jumping kicks are a favorite of many fighters and viewers. It is great to see someone fly through the air and hit his or her target. In ring or street fights, we always encounter a problem. The opponent always seems to move in the wrong direction for the one who kicks. To kick and jump in combination is surely possible, but it is strongly advised to train this only under professional guidance. All mentioned kicks, knees, punches, etc., can be made in or from a jumping position (41-44).

Jumping side kick

Jumping up high and preparation to kick

43

Jumping front kick

44

Left jumps and strikes with a right flying knee

Defense Techniques Against Kicks

Defense against kicks is done in different ways. We can categorize it by:

- blocking
- catching
- avoiding
- stopping

Blocking

Blocking techniques are in all martial arts. A block is any technique that intends to stop an attack by a counter movement where two body parts directly collide into each other. Often the "strongest" survives. You probably have seen (mostly from films and perhaps a few real examples) the harsh training methods where "fighters" hit each other's arms or legs with painful blows. Even I suffered a lot of pain when participating in such trainings. A clear example of training of this way is the wooden dummy training mainly used in Wing Chun. In this training method, a fighter stands in front of a tree-like statue called a 'wooden dummy' which has parts imitating arms and legs sticking out. The training of the fighter is to learn how to hit the arms and kick the legs to "harden" the underarms. He will do this movement hard and as fast as possible this training can be seen in many year '70-'80ies movies from last century. Bruce Lee was one of the first to show the training on the movie screen.

The question is, can you really harden your bones against blows and hits like all those "mythological" masters? To answer this question we have to look at biology. A bone is made of calcium, magnesium and many other minerals and amino acids. It is not

a solid structure, like concrete. The bone is covered by a protective shield called the bone membrane. This bone membrane is a fragile structure and can be damaged.

Although some "masters" say otherwise, it is true a Westerner is not able to harden this structure. You can change the level of pain someone is able to endure but no one can change the biological structure of the bones. But what if a bone is broken? When a bone breaks the repaired area is "stronger" than the old tissue, so if you inflict so much damage on the bones that it "breaks" all parts, it becomes stronger, right? The answer is NO; you will probably become disabled.

How do we train to endure pain? It is a slow, self-inflicted training process. A good example is the "hardening" of the shin to block low kicks. In the first stage, you start to kick a hard object softly. This way you "irritate" the nervous system. While kicking the object, be sure the area of contact does not contain any sharp parts as the focus of all power is on the smallest part of the entire contact area's surface. Step by step you move the frequency and power of the kick up until you are able to kick at almost full power (between 70% and 80%). It seems like you have hardened the shin, but in fact you have increased the level of pain you are able to endure. This way of training can be used for all other bone structures in your body.

The most painful blocking is shin on shin. The low-kick is especially famous for this (45-47). Start from the fighting position and keep your balance carefully divided between both legs. To block a kick, do not move all your weight to the standing leg. When all the weight is on one leg, it is easy to be "cheated" by the opponent. The opponent can fake a kick to one leg but actually kick the standing leg, bringing you down to the ground.

45

Basic training position

46

Left blocks a low kick with his shin (left)

47

Left blocks a low kick with right leg

To block kicks with the shin is a matter of "dry" training first. Standing in fighting position, move through the ring while lifting the legs to practice the block. Starting slow and gradually increasing speed is a very useful training method. Train every possible height for blocking. The higher your speed in the ring, the better your balance will be.

Another technique is "catching." You receive a kick (or knee or punch) from the opponent and move with the power to take most of the power out of the technique. During this movement when most of the power is neutralized, move back to the original position, catch the leg or arm and hold it. While grabbing the arm or leg, apply a holding technique as seen in the pictures 48-49 to secure the arm or leg and start returning a defensive or counter technique.

48

Right kicks and left receives the kick by locking it

49

Right receives a kick from left and locks it

A technique often seen in Thailand: a fighter delivers a kick to the side of the body (for instance a right leg kick). While the power of this kick can be devastating when it hits the target well, this time the other fighter goes along with the direction of the kick, this way taking most of the power away. At a certain moment, the fighter stops moving and receives the kick on the "open" side of the body not defended by the arms. The left arm is over the leg of the opponent. This left arm moves down and grabs the leg. Then the fighter holds tightly onto the leg against his side. After this, he returns a counter technique (a return kick to the standing leg, a knee on the kicking leg, etc.) (50-57).

50

Left holds the leg and prepares to use the elbow

51

Lefts strikes with his left elbow on the leg

52

Right takes left off balance

53

Right places a knee on the inside of left's leg

54

Right receives a kick from left and locks it

55

Right counter kicks left on the standing leg

56

Right receives a kick from left and locks it

57

Right turns over and give side kick on knee of standing leg

Sometimes you may fight against people who have slow front kicks. When the kick is supposed to land on your body, move the opposite hand and grab the heel. Now you are able to lift the leg and the opponent will completely lose his balance, or throw the leg aside and face the back of the opponent to place a counterattack.

Avoiding a kick or punch is more difficult in a ring than other techniques. To avoid a full contact kick or knee demands intensive training and a "sixth sense." You can avoid an attack by slipping backwards, diving under it or just leaning backwards; it all depends on the moment. Right after avoiding the attack, you can counterattack as the attacker is in a "weak" position.

The front kick can be avoided (58-61). When you see it coming, slip sideways or backwards. Most of the time, after avoiding the kick, a counter low kick follows on the returning kicking leg, especially when it is the front leg. At the moment it touches the ground, the body balance is not completely restored and a defense is too slow.

58

Basic training position

59

Left gives a front kick to right who blocks it

60

Right moves the kick to the side to open

61

Right counter kicks on the standing legs

A kick to the side is possible to avoid by slipping backwards when you see it coming. Most of the time one hand goes down to protect the body.

An aspect of an effective defense system is to prevent an attack in your direction. In other words, block the technique even before it starts (62-63). In Muay Thai, we often use front kicks. This kick is placed on the upper part of the kicking leg. A front kick also can be blocked by countering it before it reaches your body.

62

Basic fight position

63

Right blocks the leg of left by front kick on leg

14   KNEE TECHNIQUES

The knee techniques of Muay Thai are the sport's trademark. In the 40 years I have traveled, fought, and trained around the world, I have never found any fighting art that used the knee so effectively. For Thai, the use of the knee is more important than punching.

The kneecap is the top part of the ligament when we bend the leg. The heel must be as close as possible to the bottom. When done properly, it becomes a strong, solid weapon! This solid structure is launched at an opponent sometimes more than ten times the power of a punch. The main targets are the ribs, liver, kidneys, back, and head. A knee attack is possible at all distances.

Having a good knee technique is not enough. Clinching is made into an art by the Thai. To learn to properly clinch is only possible in an original Thai gym. It took me years to reach a state of perfection. Even now, I still find new ways, techniques, and tricks to use when fighting close. I have learned to combine the Thai way with jiu jitsu, wrestling, and MMA. The explanation of clinching in pictures is very limited, so I would like to direct you to my movies.

Knee techniques are categorized by the different directions they take to reach the target:

* **Direct knee**
* **Circular knee**
* **Close in knee**
* **Pushing knee**
* **High knee in face**
* **Flying knee**

1. The direct knee (1-6)

Take a basic stance, left foot forward. Both feet need to point with the toes directly toward the target. Make the body into a bow and the point of the knee the arrow point. To launch the ultimate force in a knee attack, the shape of the body becomes like a bow, bent to fire the arrow. The hands go toward the target to catch and pull the head down or at least disturb his or her sight.

1

Basic fighting position

2

Reaching out to catch the opponent

3

Catch the head or neck

4

Catch the "opponent" pull in and bring the knee forward

When the bow is bent as far as it can go, the knee flies in a straight line to the target. The upper body moves in the opposite direction and pulls the hands backwards. In knee actions, the opponent is not grappled and the arm position is exactly the same as when we kick. If the head or any other part of opponent's body is in the hands, it is pulled toward the attacking knee, ensuring impact is harder. Let the knee return to the original position in the same direction it came as the upper body goes back to the upright position.

5

Partner training the knee

6

Training knee on the pad

2. Circular knee (7-13)

The movement of the circular knee is best compared with executing a roundhouse kick. First the hips are opened by moving of the feet. To give a right knee, you step left and open the way for the right knee to follow. Also here the we see the bow and arrow structure occurring. In pictures 7-13 you see the steps and "bending of the bow". Also in this case the hands have a pulling effect on the opponent.

In most cases the way to place the technique toward the opponent is the same way to return to the original position. With this knee it is slightly different. When the knee lands on the opponent our bodies are very close and going back the same way is hardly possible. Most of the time the leg turns after impact, the foot goes down and is brought directly to the ground.

7

Basic training position

8

The right hits the left with the inside of the left arm

9

The right brings his second arm to enhance his position

10

After catching the right (backward standing leg) a knee follows

11

12

The right pushes left down into striking position

13

*A left knee strikes the left
(guard is down for better demonstration)*

3. Close in knee (14-18)

This is a typical Thai movement, and it seems very hard for foreigners to learn. Personally, I have probably trained this knee technique a million times.

In a fight, the opponent grabs you and you come body to body. The bodies are pressed against each other so closely sometimes that even a hand cannot fit between them. At that moment, there are only two things to do: a) start to wrestle; or b) start to use close in kneeing.

To train this technique, you need a boxing bag. The body is pressed against the 180 cm bag. Both legs are next to each other and arms around the bag. Leave no space. Then turn the right leg away from the bag and lift the knee. When the knee is at rib level, try to bring it as fast and hard as you can against the bag. At moment of impact, turn your hips in the direction the knee is going.

14

A very close training position, body is pressed against body

15

Left opens defense of right by lifting arm

16

Left start opening hips to use knee

17

Knee is turned back to striking position

18

Knee strikes on floating ribs of right while twisting hips

The return of the knee to its original position in this case is seldom the same way as it came. The foot goes straight down to the ground after impact.

Train both knees. Start with the left knee first and when it returns to the ground, move to the right side and so on. Twisting the hips is the most important part to gain maximum impact.

4. Pushing knee (19-21)

Executing this knee technique is not easy, and the power behind it seems limited. Lift the knee to the target height and let the knee go forward, straight into the direction of the target. Only upon impact does the upper body go back and the full power goes into the "kick."

It is also used is in clinching situations. Two fighters are in a clinch. One raises a knee between them and places the knee point into the body of the opponent. After the knee hits the target, the upper body moves quickly back to create space between the fighters. Having more space, other knee attacks can be made.

19

Partner stance preparing push knee

20

Lifting the knee to start a defensive action

21

The knee is placed into the body of the opponent and with force pushes the opponent away

It is also used in clinching situations where it is used or blocking the legs of the opponent. This knee is not directed straight into the opponent but in a diagonal direction. By crossing over, you disable the other fighter to make use of both legs.

The technique can be executed in two ways:

A. Using the right knee: to prevent the opponent from using his legs, the knee is placed to the left side (for opponent's right side) and the foot is held at the left side of the hip (22-23).
B. Using the same leg in the other direction, the knee is placed to the right side of the opponent's left and the foot is on the other side clinging around the hip for security (24).

22

23

Right blocks both legs with kicking cross leg

24

Some fighters execute even more specific moves when blocking the opponent. They use both legs to cling to the opponent. This is very dangerous for the fighter applying the technique and hardly possible in an open ring situation.

5. High knee in face (25-27)

A dangerous specialty of Muay Thai is a knee in the face. This knee requires a lot of flexibility, speed, and accuracy. The technique can be executed the same way as number 1 and 3 but targeting higher and using the arms to firmly pull down the opponent (25-27).

25

Training position

26

Right catches left by the head

27

Right strikes with a right knee to the head

6. Jumping or flying knees (28-29)

Jumping or flying knees are very important in different forms of fighting (28-29).

The most difficult part of this knee attack is the start of the jump position. Jumping requires an explosive power at the right moment, a great insight of the situation, and above all a perfect technique.

28

Left prepares for a jump knee

29

Left jumps and strikes with a high flying knee

15   SWEEPING AND THROWING

Sweeping seems to be an easy technique. You just sweep your foot to the ankle or foot of the opponent and let him/her loose balance. But it is not as easy as it seems. Sweeping is a matter of timing and kicking when you are in the right position.

First, these are the situations in which you are **NOT** able to place a sweeping kick:

- the moment the opponent places his full weight or most of his weight on a particular leg
- the moment the opponent moves no all the weight from the front leg, leaving it without resistance but also without impact on the total body balance

The best time to execute a sweep technique is when the opponent is moving toward you (at the moment he places his leg forward but does not yet place his full weight on it), when moving backwards and moving his balance just from the back to front leg to start the movement, and when moving around the ring. In a clinching situation, you can actually move the opponent into a position for a sweep.

In a street fight, I consider sweeping a very important way to demoralize the opponent. It is a minimum amount of force to make him lose a maximum of amount of face!

To throw the opponent, you always need to be in close contact. In Muay Thai, you are not allowed to throw. In only a few of my fights has the referee called me out for throwing, and in one fight I was disqualified because the opponent was completely knocked out after falling down from a high throwdown.

I followed Judo, jiu jitsu and wrestling training in order to learn to throw. In many ways, I consider wrestling more practical and complementary to Muay Thai than the other methods. When fighting with gloves, the practical grappling of wrestling proved to be more efficient.

In this book, we illustrate some throwing techniques that are directly linked to clinching. Most Muay Thai fighters are also interested in MMA (mixed martial arts). It is important to have at least basic knowledge of close inn fighting systems for the purpose of understanding situations such as clinching.

The most practical techniques are the leg throws. In the ring, we mainly use only three kinds. First, the leg throw that places the leg outside the body of the opponent. Looking at the pictures 1-5, you see that he stands a bit to the side of the opponent. The right leg moves away from the opponent to return at once and continue the movement when hitting the leg of the opponent. At the moment of impact, the upper body is brought to the other side and moves the opponent off balance.

1

Black shirt moves his hip into position

2

With a leg swing black shirt throws green shirt

3

Control after throwing

4

How to finish in ground position

5

In competition, you learn to inflict as much "damage" as possible on the opponent when falling.

The second technique two is executed in a clinching situation. The right leg moves around the left side of the opponent's body in a circular movement. When returning in the circle, hit the leg of your opponent. Upon the moment of impact, move your upper body forward. Fall directly with your full weight on the opponent.

The third technique is in the same close clinching situation. Your leg goes between the legs of the opponent. When between the legs, move your leg sideways and catch (when using the right leg) the left leg of the opponent. Upon the moment of impact, move your body forward and you will both fall face down to the ground (6-9).

6

Clinching situation

7

Black shirt turns his whole body around

8

9

Black shirt lifts leg between legs of green shirt

Throwing of green shirt and control position

For the next technique, we move a little higher. Your throws are now directed to bring your opponent over the hip. Going higher during the throw brings him down harder. Understanding the laws of physics is very useful here (10-13).

10

11

Clinching situation

Black shirt turns his whole body around

12

13

Black shirt lifts leg between legs of green shirt

Throwing of green shirt and control position

To throw someone over the hip, you need "grip ends," places you can grab and lift, push or pull the opponent into the movement you wish to make. The most important places are :

- around the hip
- under the shoulder
- around the neck
- under the armpits

In a close in situation, your right arm moves down. The left arm grabs the arm of your opponent and pulls him as close as possible against your own body. When finished, turn your right hip side toward your opponent. Bent both knees and go "under" the opponent while pulling. His body will go toward you and he will lose his balance. At the moment you are down and under him, move the hips up again while starting to pull your arms and hip at the same time. Your hips will move up by stretching the legs. Pulling makes the opponent lose balance and you will drop him into a circular falling movement.

At the moment you both begin to fall, bring some extra falling power with your legs by pushing off the ground. While falling, move your body on top and control the fall down. Only by doing this can you can stay on top.

When clinching, your hands and arms are moving at all times. The first thing you have to realize when fighting is that you do not have hands to grab. All techniques of throwing must be made using obvious holding points. In fact, we have two important lifting/holding points – the neck and the armpits.

When using the armpit, you have to lift the opponent to your throwing position. The most practical way of throwing an opponent is to use the lifting power of the legs when "under" the opponent. In a clinching position, your arm often will come under the arms of the opponent. To throw from this position takes a combination of speed and turning power.

Move your arm as deep as possible under the arm of the opponent into the armpit. When in, bend through both legs and turn the hips inside. Now you are standing in front of the opponent (14-19) and in a circular movement, take him to the ground.

14

Clinching stance

15

Right moves both arms under left

16

Right turns himself against left

17

Right lifts left to throw

18

Control after throwing

19

Same as 18, different perspective

When using the neck as a holding point (arm around opponent's neck) (6-9), the movement is not much different. When using the head of the opponent, it is often important to pull the opponent a bit more down and lift with the legs when in a bent position (see pics). When the opponent lands on his back, you can be sure it will greatly affect his continuation (if he isn't completely knocked out) of the fight.

An even more devastating way to throw the opponent is the "back roll" (20-24). In wrestling, this throw is a "king's" throw because when used successfully, the thrower is usually the winner.

20

Clinching situation

21

Black shirt forces green shirt to go down

22

Black shirt performs a neck lock

23

Black shirt moves down backward to throw

24

*Final after throwing in strangling∕
neck lock*

When in a clinching situation, grab the opponent in a way that both arms are locked within the hold. Then bend the knees and move backwards, pulling the opponent from his position. When moving backwards, "stretch" the knees to maximize lifting. The opponent's head is now higher than yours and will land on the ground first. Just before impact, turn your body into the upper position to finish up. When the opponent actually hits his head on the floor, he will be KO!

When training wrestling moves, I also used this throw in one fight by camouflaging the fact that it was my intention to throw (I had learned from previous experiences). It took the opponent over an hour to recover.

16 CLINCHING

Clinching is a way to move the opponent into the right position to place a knee "kick." To execute this move, the arms, hips and footwork have to be completely harmonized. The catching of the head and trying to pull it down or sideways is the core of the movement. Foot and hip work are crucial to making it all work.

Clinching is the combination of techniques to prevent the opponent's attack from pulling you down or sideways. With this, a system of attack and defense is created. In the West, we have put pinching and choking in the movements. Looking in MMA, we see throws coming from clinching positions. In this book, I show a few techniques as most are only clear when you see the actual movements on film or during seminars/lessons.

Clinching is hard to describe from position to position and is much easier to understand in an actual exercise. The pictures used here show the most used forms, but there are many more situations. Teaching clinching is not easy. The trainer needs to understand the dangers of distance. Clinching is all about the right distance to control the opponent and to execute a knee technique. Speed is important, and clinching is often based on feeling and reflexes rather than visual contact because the first thing the opponent tries to do is limit your visual possibilities. You can see this clearly in the pictures.

With the accompanying pictures I try to give inside information in the way of professional clinching techniques. It is important to follow step by step and train every movement often. Good trainers are very important to lead you to the right positions.

Series 1   Training the neck and body clinch position (1-9)

1

Start training the neck, right catches left

2

Right places two elbows on the shoulders and starts pulling

3

Left lifts up the chest

4

As last action hips move forward and strenghten the total position

5

Left catches right back around the neck

6

Left moves the left arm between the arms of right

7

The right arm is brought across the chest and face to the right

8

Left brings his hand behind the neck of right

9

The right arm of the right person is lifted and loses grip

Series 2   Crossover to free from a clinch (10-15)

10

Right catches left, arms of left are in outside position

11

Left turns arms to inside of left position

12

Right has both arms in outside position

13

Right moves his left arm over accross arms of left

14

Right keeps crossing and blocks sight of left

15

Right moves left arm back hard taking the head of left with him

Series 3   Moving like a clock (16-27)

16

Left catches right in a low position

17

Right moves hands up to the head, left goes along

18

Right starts pulling the head of left down

19

Right pushes the arm of left down

20

Right keeps on pushing arm down, his right hand starts moving

21

Right pushes his right hand in the face of left and opens guard

22

23

Left pulls down the head of right

24

Right pushes the face of left backward under nose

25

Left pulls down head of right

26

Right crosses left arms blocking the pull down

27

Right pushes back the face of left

Series 4   Arm hold / chin punch (28-31)

28

Right catches left to pull down head

29

Left blocks the pull down and crossover with right arm

30

Left turns his right arm around the arm of left

31

Left pushes his left arm into the face of right breaking right's attack

Series 5   Elbow break (32-36)

32

Right catches left to pull down

33

Left crosses his right elbow over the left arm

34

Left turns his right arm upwards

35

Right loses grip and left takes over

36

Series 6   Breaking the middle (37-41)

37

Right pulls down left

38

Left crosses over his right arm over left

39

Left turns back his right arm and brings right off balance

40

Left clinches right, right brings both arms around left's wrist

41

Right pulls back his arms, breaking right's attack

Series 7   Waving master (42-46)

42

Right attacks left

43

Left "kicks" his knee against right, bringing right off balance

44

Left attacks right

45

Right sweeps with his left leg against right

46

Left is taken off balance

17   FORBIDDEN TECHNIQUES

In this book, I show techniques that are prohibited in ring fighting. One of my past students, Willem Jan Paardekoper specialized in the combat fight techniques of KAPAP, an Israeli special forces fighting method. These pictures show a number of techniques that are forbidden in normal competition but are often used in my and our self defense lessons for police and army training.

1   Thumb-in-eye-poking

Thumb in eye

2   Knee in the groin

2

Knee in groin

3   Stamping the knee

3

4

5

Kick on knee cap

4   Front kick to the groin

6

7

Front kick in groin

5   Biting

8

9

10

Biting

6   Hitting with inside glove

11

12

Hit with inside of glove

7   Head butt

13

14

Full straight head butt

15

16

Going under the partner

17

Going up for head butt under chin

8   Beating a defenseless person

18

Punching fallen fighter in neck

19

Elbow in back

20

Kick in neck

21

Heel in side

22

Stamping on head

23

Hitting on side of head

9 Actions to the back and neck

24

Prepare to knee

25

Knee in back

26

Knee on neck

18   COOLING DOWN

Always adjust your cool-down according to the lesson. A heavy lesson needs a longer cool-down period. In a cool-down, you use many of the same movements that were used during the lesson, only at a lower pace. Keep tension on the muscles a little longer for stretching out and then let go smoothly. Unlike warming up, it is important that in a cool-down the tension is kept a little longer on a muscle group and slowly released.

In a cool-down, often a lot of stomach exercises are used. Be aware of the fact that lots of people have (hidden) back problems. Also be aware that the abdominal and lower back muscles have already been worked out thoroughly during the complete Muay Thai training.

The end of the cool-down is comprised of floor exercises with some easy stretching and, if the group is willing/able, finished off with a short meditation. Here we show some pictures of sample exercises.

1

Neck stretch to right

2

Neck stretch to left

3

Wrist training

4

Wrist training

5

Side stretch left

6

Side stretch right

7

Triceps stretch

8

Quadriceps stretching

9

Quadriceps stretching

10

Side stretch front

11

Side leg stretch sideways

12

Overstretching the back

19   TRAINING WITH A PARTNER

In this chapter, I can only outline a limited number of possible training sets. The best way to learn is to regularly change partners. You will get use to heavier, more flexible or stiff, stronger or faster, etc., opponents. It will sharpen your mind and will not endanger you.

I make a clear difference between partner training and sparring. When training with a partner, you both do the same technique for the purpose of learning. Training for different levels of students is supposed to be related to condition, fighting spirit, and technical abilities.

In my opinion, it is important to wear sufficient protection at every training (see chapter equipment). A basic set of protection for Muay Thai/kickboxing consists of:

*   gloves at least 14 oz but preferable more heavy, for woman at least 12 oz.
*   shin protectors made from a special kind of padding with Velcro straps and elastic closure, do not start to use the professional hardware right from the beginning
*   groin protector for men and women alike
*   always use mouth protector when sparring
*   hand wraps

Other things, like trousers, special shoes, ankle wraps and so on, are not really necessary.

Creativity

Fighting is not a fixed way to combat the opponent. When sparring or fighting, creativity is essential. Muay Thai used to be one fight at a time, but in recent years "tournaments" have developed. A fighter must compete not once but several times each fight night. Tactics, creativity, endurance, and stamina are the major parts needed to "play" the game of fighting.

In each session, basic fighting skills are trained. The coach must promote creative thinking and motivation for the fighter. A great way to do is through "handicap training." The coach simulates that the fighter has only one hand to fight with, or one leg is heavily injured. The fighter now must compete with only 2 or three limbs without losing tempo or variation.

Other ways to train include:

- Interval training (series of 10/15/20 seconds with 5/7/9 sec. rest)
- Streamlined training wherein one fighter attacks with a specific combination and the other counters with another combination. Both start slow and technical but increase the speed gradually
- Combination programming (for instance punch/punch/kick)
- Equipment workout, starting on the boxing bag, move to big striking pads, then to short arm pads, then boxing target pads, to end with combinations of two pads or a pad/bag combination

Mental training

Fighting and martial arts (here I distinguish between the full contact ring sports and the more traditional arts, such as karate, Judo, Taekwondo and others) have a mental target.

Enlightenment was the original goal for the ancient masters of the "arts." But in our time, we place that goal lower. Contact sport is used to release tension in the muscles and mind, decrease aggression, promote mental health stability, and most of all to eliminate inner stress.

In the "arts," there are many ways that lead to the same goal. Some take "form" in bag workouts and others in sparring. The fact is that when a person wishes to train in the "arts" to develop a healthy state of mind, we must be sure he or she approaches this road in the way that fits with his or her personality.

For teachers, it is not possible to give personal guidance when training takes place in groups. It is important that if you wish to offer the "road to inner peace" that this is clearly stated in your "commercial" information. But please be aware that in this sport, cheating is punished severely; if you do not have the ability to guide a person on "his road," do not even consider.

Basic training sessions. These are series of techniques that must return in every training.

Series 1   Left jab / right jab, right low kick

1

Right gives a left jab, left leg steps to open hip

2

Directly a right jab follows

3

A right low kick follows

Series 2   Left hook / right hook, right knee

4

Left gives left hook

5

Followed by a right hook

6

A right knee completes the series

Series 3   Left jab / right jab, mid-section kick

7

Right gives left jab

8

Directly followed by a right jab

9

Finish by a left mid section kick

Series 4   Right jab / left liver punch and right low kick

10

Basic stance

11

Right jab

12

Left liver punch

Series 5   Left low kick inside, right jab followed by left jab

13

Start with left inside low kick

14

Followed by a right jab

15

Finished with a left jab

Series 6   Step away from right jab and block, counter with knee

16

Right misses a left punch but catches the partner in the neck

17

After catching, a left knee kick follows

Series 7   Missing left jab, followed by left knee and right elbow

18

Left jab missing, pull back by catching neck

19

Directly after pulling follow left knee to liver

20

Right elbow to the temple

Series 8   Block right jab by front kick

Basic training position

Right jab attack with counter right front kick as block

Series 9   Block left jab and counter with right low kick

23

24

Left gives a left jab blocked by right

25

Right counters with a right low kick

Series 10   Counter left jab with left uppercut

26

Left lands a left jab

27

Right evades and counters with a right low kick

And the last is a long series for the more advanced students

Series 11

28

Basic position

29

Right gives a left jab on gloves

30

Followed by a right jab

31

Left conters with a left hook

32

Right follows up with again a right jab

33

And follows up with a left uppercut

34

Followed by a left knee and a group of the head

35

Right kicks left, left blocks

36

Right counters with low kick

37

Kick shown from other side

20   Trainers

A trainer is a very important person. The trainer is the person who motivates, teaches the right techniques, and assists you in training and competition. The function of a trainer is more important than he or she can imagine in the development of the mind and body of the student.

There are several different types of trainers:

- The master, who is a teacher who considers himself (I have yet to meet a woman who behaves like this) important. This trainer demands respect and rules the class like a dictator. Often we see this kind of trainer in movies. In fact, this is not the right type of trainer for the proper development of a student. The trainer hides a frustrated mind with his behavior and needs to be helped by professionals.
- The teacher. This kind of trainer wants to teach as much as possible. Every lesson is full of learning material. He speaks often and explains much. The actual training time is reduced due to his/her constant explaining. This kind of trainer wants to convince the students of his superiority of knowledge but is not really able to combine activity with explanation.
- The sportsman/woman. This type of trainer loves the sport very much and wants to be actively involved. He/she is also active during the lesson and often takes part in the lesson. He/she enjoys it so much that parts of the group do not get his/her full attention. This type of trainer is good for small groups.
- The coach. This type of trainer explains everything by talking. He/she is not willing or able (anymore) to actively show the technique. If you are able to learn through oral instructions, this can be a good trainer.
- The trainer. This person is able to actively demonstrate the technique, knows how to orally explain the techniques, and motivates you to get the maximum out of your performance. A real trainer knows who you are, what your abilities are and concentrates on how to develop the best of your skills.
- A top trainer is a person who is able to bring fighters to the top. This kind of trainer is rare. They have the knowledge to make use of special skills to improve certain qualities of their students, they are well aware of medical needs and able to mentally improve students to beyond the expected level. This kind of trainer knows how to keep a fighter strong, focused and ready. Currently, the Dutch have the best heavyweight trainers in the world.

Trainers need to develop themselves. A good trainer is always looking for ways to become better and cooperate with others. Fighting is a development, a constant

improvement of body and mind. The best trainer combines students' abilities with improvements from all other sports, like weightlifting, athletics, gymnastics, and even ballet or other dancing. Everything must be studied and used to help the student reach the highest possible goal.

When you join a gym, you join a trainer. Every trainer makes your lesson. It is important that you study the way a trainer behaves and determine for yourself if that behavior fits your mentality. Some people need a master as trainer, while others will feel very bad with that type of trainer and need a coach only. I have had students I was not allowed to touch (rape victims) so I had to be a trainer at a distance, while others needed to be physically instructed (blind students). Over the years, I have specialized in working with these specific groups and only can say that the satisfaction of trainer and student is greatest when both reach a positive result.

21　FEMALE TRAINERS

Women need a different method of training. In the fighting arts there are too few female trainers. In past year, I trained a few to become teachers in Hong Kong, Singapore, Thailand and Taipei. In the very near future, more women will enter the gym to practice fighting arts.

As mentioned in other parts of this book, it is very important that we get more female trainers, and I sincerely hope to see more of them in gyms. We need them to train our future generation of female fighters and, most of all, to help other women enjoy great training.

22   EQUIPMENT

In competitive fighting, training equipment is very important. Each piece of training equipment you use must be safe and practical for what you do. The fighting arts are cardio sports. The stimulation of the heart/lung functions is one of the most important parts of training. Another important part is the training of reflexes and correct techniques.

For Muay Thai, you will need the following equipment:

- Boxing gloves (1)
- Hand wraps (2)
- Mouth guard (3)
- Groin protector (4)
- Shin protection (5)
- Head guard (6)
- Coaching mitts (7)
- Striking pads in different shapes (8-9)
- Boxing bags in different sizes and shapes
- Clock
- Skipping ropes
- Clothing
  - Trousers (10)
  - Ankle socks
- First aid materials
  - Thai boxing oil
  - Cold packs and ice gels
  - Gel gloves

1

Boxing gloves

2

Hand wraps

3

Mouth guard

4

Groin protector

5

Shin protection

6

Head guard

7

Coaching mitts

8

Striking pads

9

Striking pads

10

Trousers

Boxing gloves are one of the most important items in kickboxing and Thai boxing. With gloves, we must distinguish between two types:

- Real boxing gloves with a fuller padding on the fist part and less padding on the back of the hand
- Kickboxing and Thai boxing gloves with a normal padding on the knuckle side and more padding at the backside of the hand

It is important to distinguish between the quality of gloves from production countries versus experienced countries. Gloves from production countries are often cheaper in price and lower in quality than those of experienced countries. The difference is in the knowledge of how to make the glove. In production countries, they follow the order of the customer and do not consider the use of it.

Gloves are made in two parts. The outer part is what you see and feel, and the inner part is the padding, a special foam. The padding must be made in layers. A professional glove has at least three different foam layers of different quality and density. A standard glove often has only two layers.

To choose a glove, you need to wear it and use it against a bag to feel how well it fits. It is not advised to feel any pressure on the fingertips, especially on the thumb. The fingers must fall behind the top sewing to create a grip when making a fist. Making a fist has to be easy, and if you have to use force all the time, it is possible to cause cramps in the underarm. A good Muay Thai glove must be able to open wide enough to grab the opponent for clinching and easy to close for punching; in other words, it must be flexible. The backside of the glove needs good padding to guard against kicks, especially to the neck and head.

Gloves are not made in sizes but weights. The size of a glove is based on the manufacturer's mall used to cut the glove. Each manufacturer has its own way and mall. A glove's weight is calculated by a multiplication of 33 grams (1oz). An official competition glove is 10oz or 330 grams. A pair must be 660 grams. Glove weighting is conducted in even numbers, such as 6, 8, 10, 12, 14, or 16oz. In the Netherlands, we use 18oz and 20oz gloves because the fighters are over 100 kg. A heavy glove is considered to be more appropriate for the sport than a lightweight glove, especially when sparring. Recently, we have decided to use no longer ounces as weight measurements but grams in order to force the manufacturers to have a correctly weighted glove. The reason for this change is because, in the past, many gloves showed an ounce weight but when weighed, it was not correct. The outer part of the gloves is made from artificial leather, PU/PVC, or real leather. Any materials are good to use. Plastics may cause more sweating than leather.

If you want to buy a glove, try it on and use it against an object or with a partner before paying.

Hand wraps are considered an essential part of the training outfit by most. It is important to know the differences between the hand wraps. A wrap is selected by:

* size of your hand; wraps are sold in lengths of 2.5, 3.5, and 5 meters
* material, such as full cotton/mixed cotton, and elastic

It is important that the wrap is long enough to cover the whole hand easily and still have enough length for the wrist. Wraps come in many colors.

Mouth guard: There are many different mouth guards:
- Simple guards. This guard is standard fit. To make it custom fit, you need to use hot water to weaken the product and shape it in the mouth by biting, sucking and cooling.
- Multi layer guards. These mouth pieces are combined with rubber/plastic of different densities and flexibilities; most are formed by the same hot water method as simple guards.
- Pasta guards. A more professional guard is made by composing different materials into one mouth guard.

When you buy a mouth guard, you have to realize that its function is not to protect the teeth but to keep the jaws closed. The jaws need to be firmly closed on moment of impact. If a hit lands on an open mouth, the jaw may be dislocated and the fragile jaw joints injured.

Groin protectors are available in many different shapes and materials. For beginners, I advise plastic protectors in a slip because they are easy to wear and clean. When you become more advanced, it is advised to get a cup with silicone sides to avoid sore skin on the inside of the legs. Metal protectors are used in competition to offer maximum protection. As far as I know, the only metal protectors available are made in Thailand.

Shin protection: In full contact sports like Muay Thai and kickboxing, the shin is a sensitive but hard weapon. We use it often to kick and block. In the past, trainers believed that it could be hardened by training without any protection. It has been proven all along that it is impossible to harden the shin, and training without protection could cause serious injuries. In the Netherlands, we developed special protection gear with extra strong foam inside (developed by Henk Kessler). After a few years, the Thai completed a prototype (developed by Fairtex/Anthony Lin) of a professional shin protector. These protectors are now widely sold and copied around the world. They are made from heavy, dense foam covered with Skintex and closed with different Velcro straps.

Head guards are worn in amateur Muay Thai competitions and by everybody under 16 years old. Hits and kicks against the head damage brain cells. Good protection is needed. It is advised to look for a type of protector that fits tightly around the head, with the ears directly behind the ear openings, and with good straps at the top of the head, behind the head and on top of the head to allow complete personal adjustment.

Coaching mitts are used to train the focus and accuracy of punches and sometimes kicks. Many different sizes and shapes are available, and it is a matter of testing and feeling what is good for your case. If you are a target puncher, you do not need to have a hard one. Power punches need to have a good, strong and relatively hard protection to protect the catcher from injuring his or her hands. A good coaching mitt has a glove on the grip side.

11

Striking pads (in different shapes) In Thailand, trainers use "paws," short arm, long, very strong striking pads made from leather and recently also from artificial materials. Training with paws is very useful to maintain and improve a good physical condition.

Besides the traditional paws, the Dutch invented the shield. This shield is a 75 x 35 x 15cm pad with four grips. There are different kinds of shields categorized by weight:

- Children's size – a special soft, but firm, padding to give the hitter a right impact and resistance but also considers the fragile bone structure of the child.
- Adult basic shield – up to 85 kg.
- Heavy weight shield – for over 85 kg.

12

Boxing bag

Boxing bags (in different sizes and shapes, sample of standing bag: 12) Since the 1970s, the fighting arts have developed rapidly and became a worldwide market. Before that time, boxing bags were made of leather and filled with all kinds of materials to give them a certain resistance. Punching the "heavy bag" was a part of every boxer's training. In Muay Thai, the use of bags is also very important for individual training.

Boxers need bags the size of a body, 100-120cm tall. In kickboxing and Thai boxing, kicks to the legs are often executed and must be trained on a bag. For this purpose, the Dutch invented a 180cm long bag made of plastic. This plastic, called byzonyl, was used to cover trucks to keep goods dry for transportation. It is a very strong and durable material.

Currently there are bags of different sizes:

80cm is used for training fast punches and elbows
100cm is used mainly for boxing and kicking
120cm is used for training all boxing, kicking and knees
150cm and 180cm are used for all techniques possible.

A good bag is filled with textiles and has a density that can be compared with the human body. A bag should not be hard. A hard bag can cause injuries. When you hit a hard object, the power you put in the punch or kick will be returned to sender.

This return power will injure you over time. The longer you train, the more chance you risk of injury. If you differ bag training between hard, medium and soft, the chances of injury is quite small. A soft bag also enables you to train wrist stability.

Bags made of leather are long lasting and do not hurt the skin, but they need maintenance and can only be made without extra stitching at the size of 180cm. The new plastic bags are also durable, easy to fill and hardly need maintenance, but it is not possible to train on plastic bags with bare hands due to their surface. When you hit the bag for awhile, the skin becomes red and finally it burns and opens up. When training on plastic bags you always need bag gloves and other protection for the bare skin.

Other bags we may use:

* Pear shaped bag – for uppercuts and elbow training
* 8-shaped bag – for uppercuts and knee training
* Wall bag – especially designed for hooks and uppercuts
* Speed ball – a ball hung from a ceiling that is used to build up endurance in the arms and shoulder, and improves eye-hand coordination
* Double end ball – for coordination and reflex training

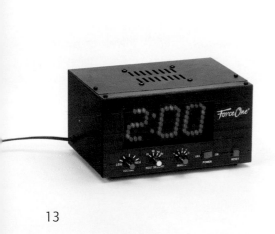

13

Clock Time is important in ring sports. A round varies between one and three minutes. In Burmese boxing and MMA, rounds can be even longer. A clock is needed to count the time of the round and the rest period of around one minute. During training, we use special box clocks, but more and more we also use interval clocks to diversify the training. An interval clock can be used to create speed differences within rounds. Original boxing clocks only are used for three-minute rounds with one minute interval rest.

Skipping ropes are important tools for condition training. The rope has been used in boxing for as long as we know. In the gym, you can find many different ropes, such as plastic speed ropes, leather with different handles, etc.

14

Clothing in the traditional fighting gym was very down-to-earth rags – short trousers, a pair of old shoes, ripped T-shirts and sweaters, and a towel. In today's gym, we see more fashionable gear. The original Muay Thai trousers only had a name sewed on it. The modern trousers are works of art. Pictures, logos and so much more complete a beautiful design or an eye-poking picture. We also see more MMA trousers used in the gyms.

Ankle socks are used to protect the ankles against swelling and to give some support.

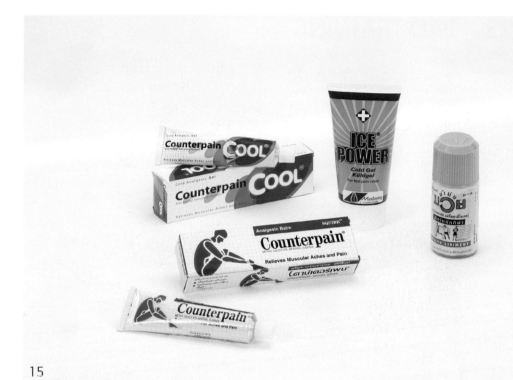

15

First aid materials: In Muay Thai and kickboxing, we use different products to comfort our muscles, relax the tension in tendons, and help in healing injuries.

- *Thai boxing oil* – an over-400-year-old formula. A strong liquid used to improve blood circulation.
- *Cold packs and ice gels* – used directly after a training. The first reaction is a lowering of blood circulation to stop swelling.
- *Gel gloves* – used to prevent knuckle injuries or when they have occurred already to help in the process of recovery.
- *Tape* – special cotton tape, 24 to 38cm to tape joints or gloves

23 PAD TRAINING

Pads or, as Thai call them, paws, are a very important instrument in training. The pads give the trainer and student many opportunities to train hard and effectively. There are three different forms of pad training:

- Trainer holds the pad, student does work out (1)
- Student holds pads and other student works out (3-5)
- Both students hold the pads and both work out (Dynamic Pad Training) (7-19)

Traditional trainer-student work-out

Basic stance for pad work out

Right kick on pads

Prepare for knee

5

6

Right knee on pads   *Training low kick on striking pad*

Pads are used in all Thai gyms. There is a difference between the way pads are used in the Netherlands and in Thailand. Thai only know the paws, which are short arm, long pads. These pads are used for decades to train every fighter. In Thailand, a fighter uses the pads in every training especially in a trainer/student combination.

In the Netherlands, we use the large pad (75 x 35 cm) often for workouts. The combination of the Thai paws and the Dutch model (invented by Henk Kessler) allows for a wider range of technical training motions (6).

In the Netherlands, we work out in group lessons. One teacher trains a group of forty or more students. Pad training is a great way to practice techniques, power, and conditioning. The workout with students is a great way to accurately exercise as it is safe for both parties. For a trainer, it is much easier to let students work out and then control/correct them.

In the double pad workout, both students hold the pads. It is a superior cardio workout for both sides. I use this kind of workout for many reasons and find it to be a superior method. I use the following methods (7-19):

- A standard technical workout – both students kick and punch the pads while holding pads on their arms at all time, an external trainer give the commands.
- A coach/student method – one pad holder is the leader and decides which techniques must be practiced. I often use this method in classes with special groups.
- Students get the command to have different techniques – For example, one student must give two jabs and a kick, and the other students follow with two hooks and a knee. Both students must be very focused on both actions.

Pad Dynamics where both work out

7

Right kick on pads

8

Left cross jab

9

Followed by right jab

10

Prepare to catch kick

11

Receive right kick

12

Right kick other side

Returning right knee

Prepare for low kick

Receive low kick

Followed by right jab

Returning left uppercut

Followed by right hook

19

Crossed by right front kick

In the situation that one student holds the pads while the other student is hitting/ kicking, we have more formulas to make the training useful in a cognitive and physical way. (20-37)

• The normal situation is that the trainer gives commands and students follow, each student practices the technique 5-10 times and then the other one will start his/her workout
• The student with the pad calls out orders he/she needs to transfer to the other student.
• The student with the pad is counter reactive and after the other kicks/punches the pad, he/she will counter to provoke a reaction.

I also use pads as a complete cardio fitness workout. In the Netherlands, we have a flow of training events to transfer people from fitness to martial arts. The person starts with aerobic combat workouts. These workouts contain all kinds of kicking and punching in the air as part of the workout. Many people like to do this for awhile and then realize that it is important to have a better technique and a target to practice on. After this air workout, they move to a bag workout such as Kick2bfit. This is a workout on a (standing) boxing bag (38-42). All kicks and punches that used to be in the air now will land on the surface of the bag giving a better direction and control.

After a while, the kicking of a standing object becomes boring and some people may want to move to a more practical implementation of techniques but do not want physical contact (yet). Pad training is the best solution to this!

20

Basic pad position training

21

Right jab on pads

22

Followed by left uppercut

23

Right jab

24

Followed by left roundhouse kick

25

Followed by a right knee

26

Then right jab

27

Left jab

28

Right low kick

29

Right jab

30

Left jab

31

Left roundhouse kick

32

Right low kick

33

Test of balance

34

Right jab

35

Prepare to receive left hook

36

Left hook

37

Right roundhouse kick

Standing bag work-out

Left jab

Followed by right jab

Directly followed by right low kick

Or mid-section push kick

24   EXPLOSIVE vs. ENDURANCE TRAINING

A fighter is explosive. Actions must be fast. In training and fighting, we learn to move in and out. Not only do we move fast but also with an explosive power. Training with weights for a fighting art or for fitness is different. In my years of working with fighters I developed different forms of training. I did my workouts with wrestlers (Piet Kanters and Henk van der Stoep), rugby players, American football pros, but most of all I learned from Arthur Mulder, an athletic trainer and physiotherapist.

His philosophy was simple and true: to throw an object from point A to point B, you need to develop an explosive power at the start of the motion. Imagine yourself as being a gun. Your fist is the bullet. If you push the fist slowly forward, the opponent has time to take a break, prepare for defense, walk away or do whatever else to make your motion useless.

Training for explosive power is training with resistance. This resistance can be a weight but also an elastic band, a spring, or even the bodyweight of a partner. The resistance must be offset by force. In weight training, the force we use is rather slow in order to get a maximum muscle stimulation effect. In explosive training, we have to put all our energy into the movement and let the movement take as little time as possible – just like a bullet.

A fighter also needs endurance but it is doubtful that he will run long distances. In Thailand, many fighters run for 10km each training day. During my study of the effect of this kind of training, I found that there was hardly any benefit to the fighter. Most fighters run with the speed of a turtle. They often do not even know how to run so they just do what is ordered and finish it off.

For a fighter, it is important to learn to use power and endurance wisely. Over the years, I discovered that a maximum of 5km is more than enough distance. You can run this distance within 20 minutes if you are fast. By doing this, you do not waste time and get a much better result. Running the 5km is a matter of building up speed. At the start, the tempo is low. Gradually, the speed is higher so you end with a sprint. In a fight, we often need to end the round or the fight at a much higher tempo than the start of the round.

In conclusion, endurance training for fighters must be chosen to benefit the quality of the training and used for a specific goal. Explosive training must be implemented at least two times a week. Explosive training sessions are advised not to last longer than 15 to 30 minutes maximum.

25   STRENGTH TRAINING

Strength training in martial arts has become a must. The principles of strength training are not the same way those for fitness training. Every resistance training is based on functional movements. Big muscles are of no use. Our muscular structure needs to be powerful, flexible and fast.

A proper strength program is built as follows:

- Basic strength
- Speed training
- Combined strength and speed training including flexibility
- Endurance strength training
- Tendon training (a new way of training for fighters)

It is important for you to know that strength training has developed a specialized way to work out and improve the quality of fighting.

26   STRENGTH TRAINING FOR WOMEN

Most women are nervous about lifting weights or using resistance when working out. The main reason that they are nervous is the possibility they will become muscular from these kind of workouts. Before starting, it must be understood that for a woman to get clearly visible muscles she will need to work out with heavy weights at least four times a week over a minimum of a year. To become muscular is not easy at all, especially for women.

Strengthening the muscles is a must when a woman wishes to compete in any form of martial arts, no matter whether it is forms or real combat. Weight training helps to make a muscle tighter, burns fat and improves contraction and speed. In short, I advise weight training to women all the time. As I mentioned in other parts of the book, weight training for women is different from that of men. Mainly the targets are different and the negative thoughts of weight work outs are evident.

Training with weights and using a dynamic form of training is entertaining and advisable. Here we introduce Functional Fitness training. This kind of training combines every movement with a practical situation. Each move mimics a practical move but by using resistance, the power, endurance and effectiveness of the move will increase.

Women can use increasing resistance, such as climbing of weights, but need to be aware of certain muscle groups, such as those within the breasts. This group of muscles cannot be under too much pressure as it will affect the size of the muscles.

27   DIFFERENT FORMS OF TRAINING

Muay Thai used to be a competition-oriented sport with the same character as K1 fighting. The brother of the Muay Thai in Burma (today called Myanmar) is still competing in tournament style. Today, we approach fighting in a professional way and compare all we do with other sports with a scientific background.

Traditional training consists of a technical section, bag workout, pad workout, and sparring. The same things are trained over and over again. Everything was built on routine. But training only with routine will make it impossible to reach the top of the fighting world these days.

The following methods are used in training:
1.   Duration training
2.   Interval training
3.   Speed workout
4.   Power and strength workout
5.   Tactical training
6.   Circuit training
7.   Periodical planning

1. **Endurance training** is a method to improve:

*   uptake of oxygen
*   lactic acids pooling and resolving that problem
*   liquid intake control
*   recuperation during active phase, stress control during activity
*   emotional control
*   determination to win

2. **Interval training:** This method has many ways of interpretation and presentation. A few examples of this way of training are:

*   normal interval – 15/30 seconds full power
*   30 seconds recuperation
*   fast interval – 15 seconds full/15 rest
*   slow interval – 30 seconds fast – 1 minute slow

Intervals are good for training power (in active phase), speed and fast power actions. Intervals are a physical form of training one's lactate levels and the best way to go fast from one biostatic phase (non-oxidative to oxidative) to the other without cramps or side effects. This way of training motivates better breathing and careful planning for how to divide power over a series of rounds.

3. **Speed workouts** are practiced with and without resistance. The resistance is a weight or elastic band, a spring, water or other apparatus. The most important part of this training is knowing proper technical execution and good ways to use resistance. Good coaching is advised.

4. **Power and strength workouts:** This training goes for the maximum level of intensity. Training with weights is a short session but every series or muscle group is trained at the maximum weight level. A power and strength workout under resistance on the bag or pads is done with the assistance of a person who supports the movements and controls the purity of the technique.

5. **Tactical training** is important for anyone training in any martial art. Tactical training also improves a person's daily performance skills in life. It is important to predict the next step of an "opponent" and learn to oversee a situation and plan for your next moves. Tactical training is strongly dependent upon one's abilities and conditioning. An example of how this works is when a slow starter competes against a fast starter, the slow starter must warm up thoroughly and start fast or concentrate on moving through the ring so the fast starter has to run after him.

6. **Circuit training** is fun for both recreation and competition. During circuit training, a participant moves from one exercise to the next. Each "station" (this is what we call an element of the circuit) has specific instructions that must be followed. A example of a circuit is:

- bag workout – 3 minutes boxing
- bag workout – 3 minutes kicking
- bag workout – 3 minutes boxing and kicking
- bag workout – 3 minutes knees
- bag workout – 3 minutes everything combined

After each 3 minutes, the person moves to the next station. A trainer/coach circulates the hall and instructs each person individually while the rest continue to work out. In the beginning, use an interval of 1 or more minutes to move from one station to the next and rest.

7. **Periodical planning** often is combined with tactical training and is determined by the season. A year is divided in seasons that depend upon when a fighter has to compete and on the level or weight. A good example for periodic training is a weight increase of 5kg to be promoted into another weight class. It is not only important to increase weight but also keep dry body mass, not lose speed, increase power and regain your fighting level. Periodical training must take place at least one time every three or four years.

28 COMPETITION DAY

For most fighters, the competition day is the one they fear the most. It is never the actual time spent fighting but the time before entering the ring. The time just before getting to the ring and entering are especially nerve-racking moments.

Each fighter is an individual. They each have certain behaviors. A trainer needs to try to understand this. Most fighters and staff are easily irritated, which is shown in a verbal way and also as behavior. It often seems that a fighter is not "in this world" due to the concentration and focus he/she experiences.

The best way to understand this day is by experiencing the moment-to-moment schedule of a competition day. In the morning, when the fighter rises from his/her bed, it occurs that today is competition day. The moment that thought pops up, concentration sets in. A fighter starts to follow a routine. He/she will start by putting on favorite clothing, eating specially prepared food, and trying to relax as much as possible. However, the harder he/she tries to relax, the more tension will build up.

When entering the fight area, several things must be done before getting into the ring to fight. Some of those things are the weigh-in session, a medical checkup, checking the round list, getting to know the referees, and checking out the area. Most fighters walk around, some sit down, and I met a few who even sleep.

Around an hour before the real fight starts, a warm-up takes place. This warm-up against the pads often sounds like a complete match. The fighter kicks and punches the pads and must be monitored by the trainer so he/she does not wear out before the actual fight starts.

Both hands are carefully wrapped in tapes, the body receives a massage, and oil is added to certain places. When the gloves arrive, these are worn with care and the wrist is taped. Most fighters wear a special fighters robe in the ring. During all this, the coach is talking to the fighter helping him/her to remember his voice. When it is time, the fighter is called to the ring. The road to the ring is always a path to fame, regardless of a win or loss.

After entering the ring, the fighter has to choose his corner and the trainer starts to prepare the fighter for the first round. The oil/fat is placed on the face near the eyebrows, cheeks and sometimes other areas. Gloves, groin protector, and mouth guards are checked and, when all is ready, the fight can start. Most fighters will express some kind of belief in a mascot, family member, or God. Most will request help in winning.

When the fighters enter the middle of the ring and they touch gloves. For a trainer/coach, the most important part of his preparation starts: he tries to voice his instructions to the fighter. Most beginning fighters hardly listen because they are too anxious. The coach/trainer is located in the corner of the ring and is able to see the fight better than the fighter, and his instructions must be followed by the fighter. However, due to the noise in the fighting arena, these instructions are hard to hear. The fighter/trainer combination is a matter of long-time training together so the fighter is able to recognize his voice in all this noise.

During the break, a fighter receives new instructions from the coach while others take care of his drinking water, cleaning the mouth protector, massaging the legs and many other things. When the bell rings, the fighter returns for the second round and so on.

After the last round, the gloves are taken off and the fighter receives the decision of the jury. When the fighter has won, often a party-like atmosphere erupts. But when the fighter loses, it is important to control the temper and emotional outburst. Losing is a hard bargain for every fighter. The disappointment and humiliation is felt deeply. At such moments, the role of the trainer and coach is very important but many trainer/coaches will drop the student, so be aware of that before starting competition.

A competition day is an emotional event for all involved. It is very important for coaches/trainers to keep a cool mind to monitor what is going on. Deep emotions are dangerous on such days because winning and losing are always close by.

29   FIGHTING WOMEN

Martial arts and ring sports were off limits to women for hundreds of years. Only in the last 20 years have women been able to train and compete. Women are an asset to the sport. But women need a different method of training than men. One of the major differences is the physical shape of the woman. A woman has more "soft spots" than a man and can be injured because of this. On the other hand, women are much more flexible in their joints and hips.

Many years ago, a Chinese woman named Jaguar To (nickname Jag) came to me for training. In Hong Kong, she was the only woman in the gym. She has a "never-give-up" personality. To become a real fighter, she took the challenge to travel to Holland nearly every month for a weekend of training. Upon arrival on Friday from Hong Kong, she took her first training and since then she never gave up. Her will to be good developed her into the first Chinese female fighter who beat a Thai KO in the ring in a first round.

Currently she runs her own gym called Force One in the major business district in Hong Kong and is still the only female gym owner in China. In recent years, I have taught an increasing number of women from all over Asia. Even in Taiwan, more and more women join the lessons.

In Europe and the USA, women have already taken a strong role in training, competition and teaching. Here we can find female trainers who combine competition with coaching. I strongly believe we have just seen the beginning of women in this sport.

30   PAIN

Pain is something we can control. Ancient masters, and even some trainers today, think pain is something that can be controlled completely. But to understand pain, we need to know what it is.

Pain is the alarm bell of your body. You need pain to tell you how far you can go and if a move is correct or wrong. Pain comes in many levels. Everyone has his/ her own level of tolerance. Training changes these levels. When you are training to increase your level of pain tolerance, your body seems to be stronger than that of general people.

I use a way of training that is used in Muay Thai. First, we kick a very hard object, such as a wooden or iron pole, very gently. The nerves are stimulated but the leg is not allowed to send pain to the brain. You have to upgrade the pain level by slowly kicking harder and harder against the object. Eventually, you will no longer feel the pain. This gradual increase of the stimulation of the nerves makes the brain aware of what is happening but forces it to tolerate the increasing level of incoming signals so it will not react to it. However, the brain will send alarm signals if suddenly the final level is reached and the bones or muscles are reaching their maximum levels. This will signal other parts of the body and cause a reaction.

We can train the level of pain tolerance but we cannot ban pain from our training or competition. Training is a tool to help us improve all our qualities and pain is needed to warn us if we go too far.

31 SPECIAL INTEREST GROUPS

Since 1979, I have used Muay Thai to help people to find a goal in life. In 1979, I was asked by the government to help with "borderline" children, kids who were completely out of control and in trouble with the police and the law. Most of the kids had been arrested for aggression, addiction, and other behavior crimes. I designed a training that was not competition related and they all started take control of their own behavior. Not one of the participants committed a crime after these lessons.

Muay Thai and kickboxing are more than punching and kicking. Training can develop:

- cognitive functions (left/right coordination, tactical orientation, etc.)
- emotional stability (instability of personality, depression, aggression, etc.)
- physical control (disabled and blind people)
- addiction control (drugs and alcohol, but also computer addictions)

Together with Kathy Houwaart and Peter de Haan, we successfully use these methods every week with customers and over the years, we have had lot of positive results.

This method can be used in traditional schools to help children understand that there are ways to release their emotions in a controlled way and behave properly.

32 SUPERSTITION

Fighters around the world have all kinds of superstitions. Some have a doll and call it a mascot. This mascot has the power of luck. Carrying the doll means he/she will have luck when the mascot is around but if the doll is missing, bad luck will emerge.

Other people have special routines before a competition or special event. They may wear a special sweater, underwear, necklace, bracelet around the arm, or any number of other items. They believe that this thing is special and will bring them luck. The belief itself is important to the fighter for his/her mental stability and feeling of security.

In Thailand, superstition has deep roots in animism. Most Thai will say that it is Buddhism, but in fact these superstitions are not related to it. A true Buddhist does not believe in ghosts but most Thai fear ghosts more than anything in life.

In Thailand, amulets with images of monks and Buddha are sold and believed that they protect the person who is wearing it. They also believe that some amulets can bring luck. Most amulets have a special gift or power that will be transferred to the owner when worn at a special place.

One clear reflection of superstition is the little ghost house in front of a person's real house. Most Thai offer incense, food and flowers to the ghost of the land and even pray for protection and security of the house and land.

Regardless of the superstition, in my opinion, we have to respect each culture for the things they believe in and how they fill parts of their life. I have always paid honor and respect to the way Thai believe. It is good to let people have their own ways and respect them.

33 SEMINARS

Seminars are important learning events. When visiting a seminar, you can learn a lot in a short time. Most trainers are not fond of students who "shop around" for knowledge but favor visits and participation in seminars, especially if given by fighters with a good name. A good seminar should have a specific topic. Every participant will be informed about the topic so he/she is able to prepare.

Seminars are given on a special day, a number of days, or even longer periods; it all depends on the topic and/or where the instructor comes from. For up-and-coming fighters and people who wish to expand their knowledge, it is important to visit a few seminars per year.

34 FINAL THOUGHTS

Starting a gym is like giving birth. At the moment your first student comes in, you realize that it is your task to guide and teach not only ways to fight but how to be a better person in as many ways as possible.

Being a good fighter is not proof that you are a good coach or trainer. In fact, as often has been proven, a good coach or trainer is often not a top fighter! To be a teacher/trainer or coach is a state of mind, a way of living, and means accepting responsibility for the future of many people.

Using this book as your personal guide for self-development is possible, but I strongly advise finding a good teacher. As a writer and pioneer in this sport, the road to gaining knowledge was long and I met many "strange" teachers with the most unscientific ways (kindly spoken) you can imagine. As most other pioneers, my body is protesting as I get older and damage surfaces.

Being a sportsman or woman, you have to realize what your target is, and always keep in mind that you only have one body and must work with it until the end of your life. Go to the extreme but realize that when climbing the hill of success there is always the other side that goes downhill. The steepness of that part of the hill must be controlled when climbing higher and higher as a mountaineer uses safety ropes while climbing. It is the task of trainers/coaches and others who guide the fighter to keep the future of the human being in mind and not the fame of today.

Muay Thai has become a million dollar (or Euro) business and to become a professional is a major goal for many who start with the sport. The road to the top is long, and the longer you wait, the harder it gets. Be aware that Muay Thai is still growing and will continue doing so for a long time.

The champions of the past are honored for their pioneering work but will they be able to compete with the champions of today? Nobody will ever be able to give that answer! We know that the sport is changing rapidly and science is becoming more important.

When you start this sport, remember to always have fun. If you are going to compete or be a trainer/coach, never lose the target of why we are working on the improvements in this sport. Focus and see that our health is the most valuable thing we have in life and training the proper way will improve it.

35   REFERENCES

Prayukvong, Kat (2006), *Muay Thai: A Living Legacy*, Bangkok, Thailand: Spry Publishing Co., Ltd, ISBN 974-92937-0-3 *Muay Thai: The Most Distinguished Art of Fighting* by Panya Kraitus and Dr. Pitisuk Kraitus, published by Mr. Panya Kraitus, Phuket, Thailand, 1988. ISBN 974-86841-9-9

Thai Boxing Dynamite: The Explosive Art of Muay Thai by Zoran Rebac, Paladin Press, Boulder, CO, 1987.

36   Credits

Coverdesign:	Sabine Groten
Coverphotos:	© Ton van der Neut
	© Thinkstock/Hemera
	© Thinkstock/Hemera
Photos:	page 11: Map of Thailand ©Thinkstock/Hemera
	page 186: monkey ©Thinkstock/Hemera
	Buddha ©Thinkstock/iStockphoto
	other photos: Ton van der Neut

These people participated in creating the pictures for this book:
1. Rene Prins, Professional boxer, Dutch and Benelux Champion Boxing, Personal Trainer, Purmerend
2. Ben van der Linden from Benny Blanco Productions, Stichting AIGHT, The Hague
3. Ed de Kruijf, former wrestler/mixed martial arts fighter, Mix Fight Westland, Poeldijk
4. Geronimo Velden, owner of Full Contact Rijswijk
5. Tim Kool and Corine Kool, owners of Gym Tim Kool, Delft
6. Jerel Wolfjager is professional freelance Trainer, The Hague
7. Jair Groot, owner of Jair PT
8. Ingemar Miguel owner of IHBC-sport, The Hague
9. Obed Groenewegen, Professional trainer and social worker
10. Yie Mee Cheung is trainer and instructor at different gyms, The Hague
11. Farid Oulad, Professional trainer at Forza Fit The Hague and owner of several gyms

37   DIVISION WEIGHT LIMITS

Division Weight Limits (WBC Muay Thai version)

Mini Flyweight
From 100 pounds (45.454 kg) to 105 pounds (47.727 kg)

Light Flyweight
Over 105 pounds (47.272 kg), but no more than 108 pounds (48.988 kg)

Flyweight
Over 108 pounds (48.988 kg), but no more than 112 pounds (50.802 kg)

Super Flyweight
Over 112 pounds (50.802 kg), but no more than 115 pounds (52.163 kg)

Bantamweight
Over 115 pounds (52.273 kg), but no more than 118 pounds (53.524 kg)

Super Bantamweight
Over 118 pounds (53.524 kg), but no more than 122 pounds (55.338 kg)

Featherweight
Over 122 pounds (55.338 kg), but no more than 126 pounds (57.153 kg)

Super Featherweight
Over 126 pounds (57.153 kg), but no more than 130 pounds (58.967 kg)

Lightweight
Over 130 pounds (58.967 kg), but no more than 135 pounds (61.235 kg)

Super Lightweight
Over 135 pounds (61.235 kg), but no more than 140 pounds (63.503 kg)

Welterweight
Over 140 pounds (63.503 kg), but no more than 147 pounds (66.678 kg)

Super Welterweight
Over 147 pounds (66.678 kg), but no more than 154 pounds (69.853 kg)

Middleweight
Over 154 pounds (69.853 kg), but no more than 160 pounds (71.575 kg)

Super Middleweight
Over 160 pounds (71.575 kg), but no more than 168 pounds (76.204 kg)

Light Heavyweight
Over 168 pounds (76.364 kg), but no more than 175 pounds (79.379 kg)

Cruiserweight
Over 175 pounds (79.379 kg), but no more than 190 pounds (86.183 kg)

Super Cruiserweight
Over 190-210 pounds (40.909 - 95.455 kg)

Heavyweight
Over 210 -230 pounds (95.455 - 104.545 kg) and up.

Super Heavyweight
Over 230 pounds (104.545 kg) and up.